CHASING LITERACY

CHASING LITERACY

*Reading and Writing in an Age of
Acceleration*

DANIEL KELLER

UTAH STATE UNIVERSITY PRESS
Logan

© 2014 by the University Press of Colorado
Published by Utah State University Press
An imprint of University Press of Colorado
5589 Arapahoe Avenue, Suite 206C
Boulder, Colorado 80303

 The University Press of Colorado is a proud member of
The Association of American University Presses.

The University Press of Colorado is a cooperative publishing enterprise supported, in part, by Adams State University, Colorado State University, Fort Lewis College, Metropolitan State University of Denver, Regis University, University of Colorado, University of Northern Colorado, Utah State University, and Western State Colorado University.

Cover design by Dan Miller

ISBN: 978-0-87421-932-6 (paper)
ISBN: 978-0-87421-933-3 (e-book)

Library of Congress Cataloging-in-Publication Data

Keller, Daniel, 1977–
  Chasing literacy : reading and writing in an age of acceleration / Daniel Keller.
    pages cm
  ISBN 978-0-87421-932-6 (pbk.) — ISBN 978-0-87421-933-3 (ebook)
  1. Reading. 2. Information technology. 3. Literacy. I. Title.
  LB1050.K395 2014
  428.4—dc23
                                              2013033546

Cover illustration © ShutterStock/agsandrew

CONTENTS

ACKNOWLEDGMENTS

I have many people to thank, not only those who supported the development of the book you have in front of you, but also those who gave so much support to me as I pursued an education and then an academic career. During my years at Southern Illinois University Edwardsville, Jeff Skoblow, Sharon James McGee, Carolyn Handa, and Isaiah Smithson challenged me as a reader, writer, and thinker. They helped me exercise my critical thinking skills and I learned so much by observing them interact with students. Their encouragement and guidance made graduate school a realistic and appealing path. Isaiah's friendship over the years has been one of the best rewards I could imagine.

I was fortunate to study with wonderful people at the University of Louisville: Anne-Marie Pedersen, Sonya Borton, Kara Poe Alexander, Tabetha Adkins, Mickey Hess, Iswari Pandey, Beth Powell, Alanna Frost, John Branscum, James Romesburg, Matt Dowell, and Jo Ann Griffin. Catching up with these friends is the highlight of the Conference on College Composition and Communication. Carol Mattingly and Bronwyn Williams stand out as dedicated and generous mentors. Bronwyn has been a strong influence on how I teach, and he has helped me develop and improve many of my ideas about the role of reading in composition. I am always impressed by Bronwyn's knack for finding the interesting idea hidden amongst the clutter and noise that so often surround it. I am thankful for all the times he helped me to do that. I also appreciate the many good conversations we've had over the years.

In my current home at The Ohio State University, generous colleagues have challenged my thinking and pointed me in productive directions. Harvey Graff gave earlier versions of this manuscript a careful reading and supplied me with thoughtful suggestions. Scott DeWitt, Louie Ulman, and Cindy Selfe helped unearth a more interesting version of the book. Their feedback has been invaluable, giving shape to so many interesting ideas and observations. I cannot thank them enough for their support. Sunny Caldwell, Liz Weiser, and Derek Boczkowski make daily academic life even more rewarding with their friendship and humor. I also want to thank the two anonymous reviewers for Utah State University Press who offered positive and thoughtful feedback, pointing me toward scholarship and ideas that opened up a few areas of the book and added strength to others. I thank Michael Spooner for being so patient, so kind, and so thoughtful. His support is precisely the kind authors want. I also thank Kellyn Neumann for her wonderful editing. Laura Furney at University Press of Colorado was patient and encouraging through the publishing process.

Tremendous encouragement has come from friends and family: Brian Cameron, Jeff Moore, Jim Steward, Kevin Jones, my brother, my mother, and my father. Finally, I thank my wife, Carolyn. Her intellectual and emotional support carried me through many days. She is an excellent writer and meticulous reader. I am so very thankful for her generous insights and endless encouragement. She is my best friend and makes each day better.

CHASING LITERACY

INTRODUCTION

Chasing Literacy argues that composition should renew its interest in reading pedagogy and research. Composition scholars have recognized how the proliferation of interactive and multimodal communication technologies has changed what it means to write in the twenty-first century. However, the counterpart to this phenomenon, changes in the purposes and forms of reading practices, has been largely unexamined by the field. This book moves toward relocating reading's place in composition with research that examines the opportunities and challenges of contemporary literacy contexts: navigating various technologies, shifting among genres and media, making meaning from a wealth of information, and alternating between reading and writing positions. These reading practices require new approaches to literacy education.

Twenty-first century literacy practices are given specific texture in this book, which employs case study research of students' reading practices to pursue the following questions: How do students read in and out of school? How do they navigate a wealth of genres and media? How do they cope with the speed of information and technological change? What do they believe about reading, about themselves as readers, and about technologies of reading? With interviews and observations of students in and out of class during their final months of high school and their first semester of college, this book provides teachers a framework for understanding the literacy challenges faced by students. At the center of that framework is the claim that speed and attention are vital components of contemporary literacy.

This research is necessary because reading pedagogy has been disconnected from the teaching of writing, with few signs of its importance at major conferences or in significant scholarship. Although composition textbooks provide suggestions

DOI: 10.7330/9780874219333.c000

for how students should read, these interventions are not the same as a sustained pedagogy that creates a language and a theory for interpreting reading situations and responding to them appropriately. Indeed, this project began from my own struggles with teaching reading, realizing that my attempts to support student reading felt like a shadow compared to the robust theory, language, and practices I possessed to support student writing. The disconnect between reading pedagogy and writing pedagogy will only grow if the field pursues writing in digital environments without considering the role reading plays in those environments as well. As we ask students to write in a variety of ways, giving them sophisticated tools for reading will strengthen how they approach and understand those genres and media.

This book benefits composition in at least two significant and related ways. First, it contributes to our ongoing interest in multimodal composition/new media writing, which has become a burgeoning area of research and pedagogy (Kress 2003; Selfe 2007; Yancey 2004). Students are being asked to create rhetorically effective texts using a range of semiotic resources. Scholars have produced numerous publications on writing theory/practice as it relates to new communication technologies and new forms of writing. Among the many topics examined by scholars, the use of image (George 2002), the use of sound (Selfe 2009), and the problems of copyright (Westbrook 2006) have been addressed. As this scholarship races forward, research on how people perceive and read new media has been overlooked (Strasma 2010). Reading research and pedagogy should be an essential part of teaching multimodal composition: students who are more critically and rhetorically engaged as they read new media are likely to be more thoughtful composers of it. We are giving students frameworks for perceiving the writing that occurs in new media contexts, and we are creating pedagogical tools for teachers. We need frameworks and tools for new media reading as well. With this book's focused look at how students perceive and enact reading in different contexts with different media, it moves toward this goal.

Second, paying attention to reading can add to our understanding of how the rhetorical canon of delivery has changed with new media. A common problem associated with contemporary reading is information overload. Although Geoffrey Nunberg (1996) notes that "[t]here has always been too much to read" (126), he argues that the expansion of digital texts on the web has created a different situation for modern readers: the open publishing of the web makes the number of texts "genuinely unprecedented," and the open and easy access to information only increases "the impression of overload, rather than relieving it" (126). However, I argue the "overload" problem is more layered than that, involving both form and content. Readers face not only a huge number of texts, but also a great variety of texts. That is, the packaging of communication comes in so many varieties that readers often navigate unfamiliar genres, specialized discourse, and different combinations and arrangements of media. Because of our many communication options, scholars have revived the rhetorical canon of delivery for digital contexts (Welch 1999; Porter 2009). A focus on reading can help us understand how people want to access texts— how they want them delivered—and how they learn to construct texts from a range of delivery choices. In the book, I examine participants' reading and writing practices and offer concepts such as acceleration and ephemeral rhetorics to help explain delivery choices. This research can contribute to further investigations into how delivery relates to new media reading/writing, and it can aid teachers in helping students learn how to approach a variety of reading and writing situations.

These two benefits are at the heart of this book, and I approach them with the argument that speed and competition for attention are defining features of contemporary literacy. A challenge for students and teachers is to confront and make use of the accumulation and acceleration of literacies that influence how people understand and engage in reading and writing practices.

ACCUMULATION AND ACCELERATION

We can begin to understand modern reading challenges by examining how the vast expansion of genres and media has increased the range of literacies while also demanding more of those literacies. These new technologies offer individuals easier access to a wider array of information, to more forms of communication, and to larger audiences than ever before. At the same time, these new technologies and practices ask more of people if they wish to keep up as students, as qualified workers, and as informed citizens. In other words, we embrace the wealth of information and the technology options available to us, but we also feel overwhelmed. A new cell phone or reading device presents another learning curve. Office workers gain new capabilities with the latest software, but they have to adapt to the changes that come with the update. A quick Google search results in millions of hits with dubious reliability. More and more job applications go online, even if the jobs themselves do not involve computers. The latest research offers new perspectives, but keeping up with that research can be overwhelming.[1]

This paradox of literacy—that it enables and demands, that it increases in scope and can overwhelm in practice—is a central concern of this book. Indeed, writing teachers have more kinds of literacy to draw on in the classroom, which presents an opportunity to reach more students and to help them navigate the genres and media they will encounter in their daily lives, but it is also a challenge for those teachers to keep up with the latest literacy development or to choose among the many inroads to reading and writing. These opportunities and challenges present themselves every time we craft a syllabus. Do I include a visual assignment? A podcast or a video essay? Do I cut a reading or a traditional essay assignment? Should I have students critically examining Facebook and Twitter? We may feel as if we are constantly chasing literacy.

The expansion of genres and media is a part of what Deborah Brandt (1995) has called the "accumulation" of literacies, which consists of the "piling up" of old and new literacy materials and expectations as well as the "spreading out" of literacy's influence on more parts of our lives. Brandt derived the concept of accumulation from interviews that covered twentieth century changes in reading practices; she drew important twenty-first century implications from the concept in the early 1990s, as the World Wide Web emerged and grew into a daily literate experience—and well before the significant developments of Web 2.0, which have drastically changed how we share and receive information.[2] Brandt's concept of accumulation is crucial for studying contemporary reading, and I add to it by examining recent techno-cultural developments that have created new rhetorical and literate contexts. I argue that we can best understand reading by examining how it is influenced by what I call a culture of acceleration: literacy is tied to educational, business, social, and technological contexts that value speed and increasingly enable and promote faster ways of reading and writing.

Brandt's examination of twentieth century literacy experiences reveals two significant developments. First, she notes how literacy became interwoven with more domains of daily life throughout the century, "reorganizing an array of economic, legal, political, and domestic activities. The increased powers accorded to print have sharpened the need for reading and, increasingly, writing to navigate life" (Brandt 1995, 652). This is the "spreading out" aspect of literacy's influence on life domains as well as the influence those domains have on literacy; literacy takes on multiple forms used to perform daily activities, and, as those activities adjust to social changes, so do the forms of literacy. As Brandt observes, this "unprecedented" feature of modern literacy learning creates "challenges faced by all literacy learners in a society whose rapid changes are themselves tied up so centrally with literacy and its enterprises" (651). These rapid changes participate in the culture of acceleration, simultaneously responding to and contributing to the increasing demands on readers and writers.

Connected to the horizontal "spreading out" of literacy is the second development, literacy's vertical "piling up" of multiple forms of reading and writing. As social changes influence and are influenced by changes in literacy, collections of fading, ongoing, and emerging forms of literacy pile up as texts and practices. Some of these forms persist in "residual" ways, "as materials and practices from earlier times often linger at the scenes of contemporary literacy learning" (Brandt 1995, 652). Emerging forms often take on aspects of fading and ongoing literacies, reformulating older practices for current and future social needs. Brandt reflects on the consequences of these old, current, and new interactions: "These complicated amalgamations of literacy's past, present, and future help to formulate the interpretive opportunities and complexities facing current generations of literacy learners" (665). This is the paradox of contemporary literacy: as opportunities expand for how we can receive and communicate ideas, that expansion creates an ongoing challenge to adapt, to (re)situate ourselves as users of literacy among reconfigurations of old, current, and new literacies.

This ongoing challenge can be illustrated by two brief examples, one from publishing and one from teaching. Best-selling novelist Scott Sigler spent twelve years attempting to get published. Then, in 2005, he became one of the first authors to release his fiction for free in the form of serialized downloadable audio files, or podcasts. He also used other media—video advertisements for the books, e-mail, and instant message communications with fans—to spur interest in his work. The popularity of the podcasts led to a five-book deal with Crown Books, with the first published in 2008 (Lewin 2008). The piling up and spreading out of literacies allowed Sigler multiple channels for communicating with an audience and building a fan base—channels unavailable to would-be authors before the web and the rise of social media. However, the proliferation of literacies was also a cause of Sigler's extraordinary efforts: competition among media for people's attention has increased demands on writers and publishers to gain that attention for print books. Writers less savvy with new media may be unable to reposition themselves in a digital age as both print and new media authors.

Composition teachers should have no problem seeing the piling up of materials and practices in their classrooms and on their syllabi. Think of the composition classroom before and after computers, with the arrival of these machines leading to pedagogical opportunities (the advantages of digital editing) and challenges (the time devoted to functional computer skills). Then, the computer becomes networked, adding hypertext code and web design to the goals of literacy. As various forms of reading and writing emerge on the web—e-mail, blogs, wikis, discussion forums, tweets, chats, etc.—the available resources for communication expand in the composition classroom. Persisting throughout these developments is the form of the alphabetic print essay, valued for its tendency to support extended thinking and for its institutional currency. These brief glimpses at historical moments in composition suggest fading and emerging literacies, and the opportunities and challenges that accompany them. Threaded throughout these moments are teachers and students, (re)situating themselves among the literacies piling up and spreading out around them.

As literacies accumulate and as new forms appear, keeping up is vital. As Brandt states, the ability to use literacy "at the end of the twentieth century may be best measured as a person's capacity to amalgamate new reading and writing practices in response to rapid social change" (Brandt 1995, 651). Brandt points to the importance of speed in this piling up and spreading out. However, I argue that speed as an influential force has become a defining feature of literacy change since her work. This is due to the rise of a culture of acceleration, a gathering of social, educational, economic, and technological forces that reinforce values of speed, efficiency, and change. Literacies are bound up in and tied to these forces, so as these forces influence cultural changes, literacies change with them. Because these forces are aligned with values of speed, efficiency, and change, literacy also moves in those directions.

Acceleration occurs in two related ways. First, in the smaller sense, literacy technologies and practices tend toward speed. That is, they aim to achieve some end faster. Second, in the large sense, literacies can accelerate: appearing, changing, merging with other literacies, or fading at a faster rate. For instances of literacies appearing, one must only think of the fact that MySpace, Facebook, and Twitter all arrived within a three-year span, 2003–2006, and quickly became popular literacy practices. A form of literacy can rise to importance and fall out of practice in a short amount of time. For instance, knowing how to use hypertext markup language (HTML code) was an important aspect of electronic literacy in the 1990s, but is now fading. Some teachers may recall developing pedagogies around multiuser domains (MUDs), Second Life, and MySpace; these, too, have largely faded. An established form of literacy may remain but in an altered form. E-mail was a dominant form of electronic communication in various life domains, but has lost most of its social use to Facebook and texting, leaving it to fulfill the more formal communication needs of business and education. As literacies remain, they change: web browsers have moved from multiple windows to multiple tabs for multitasking purposes and continuously offer extensions to control more of the online experience; Facebook continues to update its functions and appearance; and cell phones have added keyboards for faster texting, application software (apps) for specific tasks, and speech recognition and activation software (e.g., Siri for the iPhone).

A significant effect of accumulation and acceleration is that what counts as effective reading and writing becomes a moving target—over time and from context to context. People in various situations must keep up with the latest changes, whether they involve using Facebook for social purposes, employing social media for workplace goals, or learning the latest course management software. Literacies are increasingly tied to contexts that value and reinforce speed and brevity. Much has been written to disparage "fast literacies" such as text messaging and multitasking, with the implied or openly stated conclusion that education should provide a bulwark against these anti-intellectual practices (Carr 2010; Edmundson 2004; Faigley 2006). I respond to some of these criticisms throughout the book and articulate a nuanced, productive relationship between "slower" and "faster" forms of literacy. If we take accumulation and acceleration as defining features of contemporary literacy, then a goal for educators should include helping students gain versatile, dexterous approaches to both reading and writing so they are prepared to navigate a wide range of ever-changing literacy contexts.

THEORY AND METHODOLOGY

To understand modern reading situations, I wanted to gather a detailed sense of students' literacy practices, which were examined in three contexts: high school, college, and home. Longitudinal research has shed some light on how students develop as readers and writers over their years in college (Carroll 2002; Sternglass 1997), but composition has not done much work on the transition to college (Harklau 2001; Reiff and Bawarshi 2011). This transition should be of interest to writing teachers; after all, many first-year composition students were in high school only a few months before they walked into our classrooms. Because I was interested in the reading practices students brought into college, I wanted to examine that transition. I also wanted to interview and observe students at home to get a better sense of how they perceived and enacted reading outside of school.

Case study research was the most appropriate method for gaining the kind of in-depth attention to the life histories, home and school settings, and participant viewpoints necessary to understand complex literacy practices (Dyson and Genishi 2005). Although case studies are limited by their small size, they have the advantage of being able "to illuminate the general by looking at the particular" (Denscombe 2007, 36). I interviewed and observed student participants in 2006 during their final months of high school and their first semester of college. Nine participants from a Midwest high school were involved in the high school portion: Mark, James, Sarah, Lauren, Nadia, Amy, David, Tim, and Diana; the final four remained for the college portion.[3] I interviewed them multiple times, gathering literacy histories (Barton and Hamilton 1998) and often asking the same questions at different times to see if and how responses changed. During interviews and observations, I took field notes and audio recordings, which were transcribed and coded for themes that would frame follow-up interviews. Interviews with the director of the library, a senior English teacher, and family members of four participants allowed fuller understandings of the participants and their home and school environments. Finally, and most importantly, I checked my interpretations against my experiences and knowledge as a teacher and scholar of literacy. Significant observations made throughout the book were "tested" in a sense by my teaching experiences with hundreds of students.

Research participants always offer a limited set of perspectives on complex phenomena, and these case study participants are no different: the nine middle-class students who attended an above-average high school may seem familiar to some readers and unfamiliar to others. Obviously, they do not represent all students. Most of the participants considered themselves to be good students and good readers; however, even the "good students" struggled with elements of college reading. Although the participants engaged in typical teen media use—reading the web, participating in online social networks, sending text messages—only one made an attempt to produce complex online content. The interviews and observations, particularly those conducted in the students' homes, revealed thoughtful and complex online reading practices.

This research was informed by the "social turn" in literacy studies: instead of seeing literacy as a set of discrete skills, the sociocultural view acknowledges multiple forms of literacy and the influences upon literacy by social, cultural, economic, and political forces. New Literacy Studies (NLS) is founded on this principle (Lankshear and Knobel 2003; Street 1995), which takes literacy to be more than the decoding and encoding of text; instead of one literacy, we have literacies that take into account diversity of language and culture as well as expressive modes offered by various media (Kress 2003). Recognizing multiple literacies, composition and literacy scholars no longer limit reading and writing to the printed word. In this book, literacy is associated with—but not limited to—alphabetic text. Indeed, because written words are so familiar, we often forget they are symbols, just marks and squiggles on the page and screen. We communicate through symbols, whether those symbols are words or images. Literacy is a means for creating and interpreting meaning, an act of semiotic communication. When defining reading for this study, I preferred that alphabetic text be involved in some way. When words and images combined to make meaning, I considered that reading. If a video game screen had no textual accompaniment, I did not consider that reading.

Acts of reading and writing are shaped by their social contexts. Schools, homes, workplaces, and public spaces—within and among these life domains (Barton and Hamilton 1998), different kinds of reading and writing are valued, which means that being a different kind of literate person in each domain is valued. These domains are influenced by and influence larger cultural, economic, political, and historical forces. This perspective on literacy is necessary to study and appreciate the complex literacies demonstrated by the participants in this study. One rich area of discussion in NLS research involves the relationship between local and nonlocal (or remote, or global) contexts. By focusing on the local contexts in which literacy practices take shape, literacy theorists and researchers avoid unidirectional, autonomous causes and explanations for how literacy develops and gets used. Although this shift to the local has been an essential move for NLS, some scholars have recognized the need to pay more attention to how local and nonlocal influences interact (Brandt and Clinton 2002; Collins and Blot 2003; Street 2003). As Stephen Reder and Erica Davila (2005) state, "Though NLS was founded on the idea that local context must be the focus of research on literacy as a situated social practice, advocates have recently emerged for a shift in focus to include the broader ways in which literacies pattern in society" (177). Even though NLS research and theory has been capacious enough to consider both local and nonlocal contexts, more theoretical frameworks are needed to understand how the nonlocal might influence those patterns.

Brian Street (2003) argues that all local-nonlocal interactions result in "hybrid" literacy practices: "The result of local-global encounters around literacy is always a new hybrid rather than a single essentialized version of either. It is these hybrid literacy practices that NLS focuses upon rather than either romanticizing the local or conceding the dominant privileging of the supposed 'global'" (80). Without privileging the nonlocal in this book, I do give the nonlocal specific consideration by discussing how literacy beliefs are shaped by cultural narratives (chapter two) and developing acceleration as a powerful influence on the "ways in which literacies pattern in society" (Reder and Davila 2005, 177). Although I regard acceleration as a powerful force that can influence tendencies in literacy practices, I do not regard it as determining what people do with literacy. Even when nonlocal forces exert powerful influence, people remain individual agents who develop and use literacy within specific domains of life, responding to and even influencing the shapes of literacy at home, at school, and in their community.

OVERVIEW

Chapter one examines reading's relationship to composition. Drawing on the work of Patricia Harkin (2005), David Jolliffe (2003), and Mariolina Salvatori and Patricia Donahue (2012), I argue that reading research and pedagogy have become marginalized in composition. This marginalization has limited composition's ability to achieve a fuller understanding of twenty-first century literacies: even though composition has moved forward with studying and teaching new forms of writing, it has left new forms of reading unexamined. If we accept that reading and writing are related acts of meaning-making, and if we want a more thorough understanding of contemporary writing, then new forms of reading need to be a part of the research agenda on new forms of writing.

Chapter two explores the connection between accumulation and values-conflict by examining the participants' perceptions of reading in and out of school. Their perceptions of literacy are important because people's beliefs about literacy affect what they do with literacy. Even though the participants read a wide range of media, they expressed a limited view of what counted as reading. Interviews with the participants revealed a tendency to devalue their digital literacies, associating them with pop culture and even using the same dichotomous language found in cultural narratives that distinguish between "high" and "low" culture. I argue that cultural narratives about literacy are a strong influence upon literacy perceptions, and I elaborate on the concept of accumulation to offer an explanation of how value-imbued narratives get attached to literacies as they spread out into various domains. I then explore how these values can cause conflict when teachers and students have different expectations for reading and writing in college.

Chapter three examines the pressures of and responses to accumulating and accelerating literacies at home and at school. I draw on the work of Manuel Castells (2010) and Robert Hassan (2009) to argue that acceleration is a defining feature of contemporary literacy, which values and reinforces speed and efficiency. For the participants, accumulation and acceleration seemed to contribute to a cluttered, rushed curriculum at school. In their daily social lives, the convenience of instant information and fast social interactions through technology also brought the pressures of information overload and the expectation of constant social availability. I discuss James Porter's (2009) conceptualization of digital delivery, the components of distribution and circulation in particular. In my examination of the participants' delivery choices in online social networks, I observe that the participants were more concerned with distribution (the initial packaging of a message) than circulation (how that message might spread); the participants engaged in ephemeral rhetorics, brief messages aimed at gaining attention and then fading away.

Chapter four focuses on three participants' reading practices at home as they navigated online environments. I examine how the participants multitasked and made conscious choices about how to direct their attention. Many scholars have talked about the importance of attention in an age of information overload (Lanham 2006; Lankshear and Knobel 2003), but I argue that attention cannot properly be understood without accounting for literacy acceleration. This chapter briefly responds to popular criticisms of multitasking and attention (Carr 2010) and points to more productive perspectives. The interviews and observations lead to a heuristic for studying and teaching multitasking in complex online environments. In addition, I observe a form of reading called *foraging*, a purposeful wandering across texts that involves gathering materials and ideas. Finally, I explore how the participants oscillated between slow and fast reading, with varying attention.

Chapter five turns to the relationship between reading and writing. I examine the participants' experiences of reading and writing in college, reflecting on how they struggled to productively connect the two acts. Then, I turn to Brandt (2009), who argues that the reading-writing relationship has changed in recent years: first, our reading-writing technologies position people so they are more likely to shift from reader to writer; second, mass writing is now in contention with mass reading, overshadowing the importance of reading in some aspects of life. Regarding the second point, I provide an alternative view based on two participants' online writing practices, which were promoted by sites that provided models and support. I contend that such examples mark a cooperative aspect to the reading-writing relationship. I explain how accumulation, acceleration, and the social aspects of the web contribute to these writing practices.

In the conclusion, I open with the question "What does it mean to be a reader in the twenty-first century?" I reflect on important observations from the book to offer a sense of the challenges and opportunities for literacy learners resulting from accumulation and acceleration. After observing that current composition pedagogy does not account for these challenges and opportunities, I offer a starting point for reading research and pedagogy with a detailed discussion of four significant features of contemporary literacy that emerged from the study: accumulation and curricular choices; literacy perceptions; speeds of rhetoric; and speeds of reading.

NOTES

1 Corporations, law firms, and public institutions have a growing need for information managers to preserve, organize, and keep track of documents (De Aenlle 2009). A growing industry is focused on "data analytics," helping companies analyze and use data for improved business decisions. IBM estimates its analytics business will "grow to $16 billion by 2015" (Lohr 2011).

2 In March 2003, only 100,000 blogs were found by Technorati, the best blog-tracking service. Within the next year, more than 4 million blogs were found. Today, over 100 million blogs exist worldwide (Lessig 2008, 58).

3 All participants have been given pseudonyms. The study was approved by the Institutional Review Board (IRB). For more information on the participants and my methods, see Chapter two and the Appendix.

1

LOCATING READING IN
COMPOSITION STUDIES

*"[W]hat an instructor believes about reading is an essential
precondition to organizing and teaching in a writing classroom."*

—Marguerite Helmers (2003, 4)

David and Diana could not have been more different as high
school students: David struggled in many of his classes, especially when it came to reading. He passed with average grades,
and he had to work to achieve those average grades. In classes
that involved reading, David was quiet and lacked confidence.
As David put it, "I'm bad at reading. I don't know if I need more
vocabulary or a speed reading course, but I don't like it, and
I'm not good at it. Others [read] faster and get more out of it
than I do." Diana, on the other hand, excelled at reading and
in her classes in general. She often participated in class, confident that she knew the material and knew the right things to say.
According to Diana, "School's not that hard. I'm busy, and I've
got a lot of homework, but I do fine. I have a lot to read, but I
just do it." For Diana, school was not a matter of struggling to
get by but of striving to maintain a level of excellence.

In college, David struggled even more with reading, and
Diana found that her usual ways of reading did not work anymore, noting that "they [teachers] expect us to do different things in different classes with reading." Although Diana
remained a good student, she felt frustrated by these unclear
expectations and her lack of preparation; she didn't struggle,
but she didn't know how to excel. These two students suggest
the range of students that come into our first-year composition
(FYC) courses: the struggling students, uncertain and quiet as

DOI: 10.7330/9780874219333.c001

the class discusses a reading, stumbling over a word or even drifting off as they try to make a point; and the above average students, those who seem confident but end up skimming the surface of a reading for "the point" and do not see it as a complex, layered event. The students in this study went to a high school that performed exceptionally well on state tests; it was held in high esteem by parents, teachers, and students. If these students experienced difficulty with reading in college, then what does that suggest about the place and purpose of reading pedagogy? For far too long, reading pedagogy has been aimed at students like David, those who struggle, those who might need remedial education. But what about Diana and her overachieving peers? What about the students who seem to read well, but lack flexible strategies or an appropriate critical stance? How might we pursue research and pedagogy that would benefit a range of students? And, most importantly, what pedagogical possibilities are we overlooking by not investigating reading at a time when reading has so many rich manifestations? In their statements that opened this chapter, David and Diana referred to their proficiencies with traditional print literacies in high school and college. As we will see throughout the book, the participants generally viewed digital literacies as non-school practices. Might David have been more confident as an academic reader if his experience with digital texts had been drawn upon? How might have Diana and David engaged their reading and writing practices in richer, more connected ways in school through exposure to a range of literacies?

This chapter examines composition's relationship to reading. Although literacy studies has shaped compositionists' approach to writing instruction, it has made less of an impact on our thinking about reading in the writing classroom. Reading pedagogy, however, is crucial to the work of writing instruction. As Marguerite Helmers (2003) observes, "what an instructor believes about reading is an essential precondition to organizing and teaching in a writing classroom" (4). The beliefs we have about reading, and the view we have of our discipline's relationship to reading, shape what we do with reading (and writing) in the classroom. As reading and writing take on more shapes and purposes—as they accumulate—in the twenty-first century, how prepared are we to engage new literacies if we leave reading in its largely invisible state?

READING'S PRESENCE AND ABSENCE

Consider the curious double life of reading in composition classrooms. All at once, reading is both invisible and constantly present. It seems to constitute so much of what we do in the classroom, yet it may also be one of the least theorized parts of classroom practice. We see reading most when it goes awry: when students stumble over words, when they offer up an interpretation that makes us wonder if we're all reading the same thing, when they read for the quick answer instead of the deep connection, when they simplify an author's position. But, for the most part, reading leaves no trace—no drafts, no revisions, no peer review, no individual conferences.[1] When it seems to go well—or at least when it doesn't derail the goal of teaching writing—it drifts into the background, a ghost of a concern.

Reading's simultaneous presence and absence can be seen in Pat Hoy's (2009) description of how he used to teach reading and why that changed. Hoy states that he had "developed a pedagogy that would not require [him] to teach students how to read" (305). That is, students learned particular ways of reading through assignments and exercises, not from a more direct form of instruction. When that pedagogy was successful, he was "left free to teach writing, not reading" (305). But in recent years, Hoy's students were not reading the way he expected, and he found he was not alone: other teachers in his program all agreed on the "pervasive" reading problem and its characteristics (305). I think Hoy's initial view echoes what many composition teachers desire: students should either "already know how to read" or learn how to read for college as a byproduct of other assignments through a kind of pedagogical osmosis. We expect certain kinds of reading in our classes, and we want that reading to be invisible, automatic, and ready to serve writing. When reading becomes visible, when it requires new scaffolding, then the reading-writing balance of the classroom is upset. Hoy and his colleagues are certainly not alone in feeling dissatisfied and even frustrated with student reading. In their analysis of students' writing from sources, Rebecca Moore Howard, Tricia Serviss, and Tanya K. Rodrigue (2010) found that students seemed to engage minimally with sources. Based on the students' lack of summary and their focus on individual sentences from sources, the researchers raise questions about students' reading practices and "ask not only whether the writers understood the source itself but also whether they even read it" (186). As they note, their "preliminary inquiry suggests that we have much more to learn" about how students read and use sources (189). The research by Howard, Serviss, and Rodrigue is an early stage of The Citation Project, a large-scale empirical study of how students at multiple schools use sources in their writing. The Project recognizes that we do not have much empirical data about how students actually engage with sources. At my institution, which is comprised of a selective-admission main campus with open-admission regional campuses, an assessment of FYC research papers from every campus found a common problem of minimal and incorrect source use. Writing from sources is a complicated act with many interrelated parts, but how much of the minimal source engagement stemmed from unsophisticated reading, and by extension, from underdeveloped reading pedagogies?

Because the teaching of reading in college composition classrooms has received little attention in recent years, teachers lack the pedagogical theory and practice with which to assist students with their reading.[2] First-year composition students then lack the reading strategies and the metacognitive awareness that could help them adapt to the reading and writing situations they will encounter in college and beyond. Being immersed in composition scholarship and having taught students at different universities and at different levels of college preparedness, I have a wealth of resources to draw upon when teaching writing. Reading is a different story. For many years while teaching reading, I turned to a textbook and assigned reading questions, journal entries, and reader responses. In the absence of a theoretical basis, however, these acts felt like an imitation of real teaching, and I struggled as a teacher when students struggled as readers. In addition to having little theory and little language for reading pedagogy, I also had little idea who the students were as readers. What do they read at home? What kinds of reading did they do in high school? How do they read with technology? The questions generated by those difficult teaching days led to this research. My call for a renewed interest in reading would be well deserved, even in a print-dominated world. However, it is even more urgent with the challenges and opportunities posed by rapid technological change.

Reading and writing have changed. We see this every day. Computers and the web have profoundly influenced how we approach texts, shifting between the position of reader one moment and writer the next (Brandt 2009; Lessig 2008). Alongside this shift, dynamic and rapidly changing literacy practices continue to expand the range of genres and media that we encounter and manipulate. Contributing to and navigating among this wealth of texts means we learn and adopt different ways of reading and writing. We are no longer passive consumers, if such creatures ever existed: more than ever, we are participants in how media are produced, distributed, and accessed. Composition has responded to such changes by expanding what it means to write, yet the corresponding literacy practices—how we read digital texts—have received less attention.

One notable call to attend to new forms of composing appeared in Kathleen Blake Yancey's (2004) address at the Conference on College Composition and Communication (CCCC), in which she asserted that composition needs to recognize that the writing we teach in school is becoming more distanced from what students do outside of school: "Never before has the proliferation of writings outside the academy so counterpointed the compositions inside" (298). Yancey's recommendations for change include bringing "together the writing outside of school and that inside" (308). She emphasizes the "circulation of texts" aspect of the new curriculum, which has students writing outside of the student-to-teacher model and transforming pieces of writing across genre and media: "As they move from medium to medium, they consider what they move forward, what they leave out, what they add, and for each of these write a reflection in which they consider how the medium itself shapes what they create. The class culminates with text in which they write a reflective theory about what writing is and how it is influenced or shaped or determined by media and technology" (314).

Yancey's proposal is important because it sets a new agenda for composition, but it is also interesting in the fact that the agenda is not so new (as Yancey herself acknowledges). The basis of this agenda was formed by the work of literacy scholars, particularly the New London Group (Cope and Kalantzis 2000), who argue for a semiotic view of communication: rhetorical and material contexts influence how people choose from a range of modalities—text, sound, image, etc.—as they design and deliver signs; in making signs, they reciprocally draw from and contribute to the semiotic resources available. Similarly, Yancey's "circulation of texts" model asks students to consider how to write with different media, thinking about and using appropriate modal resources in particular situations. Yancey and the New London Group ultimately want students who are more than just technically proficient with technologies: they want students to cultivate an aware, dexterous mindset that can respond to different situations with critical, creative literacies. Given the fast-changing nature of literacy, should we not aim to cultivate the same from students' reading practices?

Composition is right to respond to new literacies with research and pedagogy adapted to new ways of composing. However, the field's response should also include attention to new ways of reading. In turning to visual rhetoric and multimodal composition, we must make a concerted effort to consider how reading happens across semiotic domains, with print text remaining an invaluable part of contemporary literacy practices. The role of reading is crucial for articulating a more robust understanding of new literacies. Kip Strasma (2010) argues that we need a "new epistemology of reading new media that avoids the pitfalls of now-forgotten inquiries into hypertext and its related field of theory" (183). So far, early hypertext scholarship and early new media scholarship "parallel one another in that those early works focused on theoretical concerns rather than empirical and epistemic research, and, similarly, that work neglected classroom specifics and empirical research on individuals or groups of readers" (192). Strasma's warning is well taken, and this book aims to fill the gap with research and a pedagogical framework that considers an expanded sense of how reading happens, how reading can be taught, and how reading can be explicitly connected to writing in productive ways that reflect the dynamic range of contexts and media in which students will read and write.

READING'S STATUS IN COMPOSITION

As writing teachers we have a pedagogy based on a model of growth: we start from where the students are and use appropriate exercises and assignments to help them develop as writers, asking students to write in different genres and for various audiences to reinforce the situated, contextual nature of writing. We have a wealth of tools, practical guides, and theoretical scholarship that prepare us to help students become self-sufficient writers. We actively see students as writers, and we encourage students to see themselves as writers: to develop processes, to cultivate voices, to draw in and engage with audiences. We teach writing as a way of thinking. These are the values we have attached to writing and that we emphasize in our pedagogy. We have a tradition, a disciplinary identity formed around the power of writing and the potential of writing to effect change. I find little evidence of a similarly well-developed approach to reading pedagogy.

The title of David Jolliffe's (2003) "Who is Teaching Composition Students to Read and How Are They Doing It?" poses an appropriate question, given the lack of attention to reading

pedagogy in the major journals, books on composition pedagogy, and the field's flagship conference, CCCC. Jolliffe's examination of the 2003 CCCC reveals that in "the 574 concurrent
sessions, workshops, and special-interest group meetings [. . .]
the word *reading* appears only twice" (128). The 2005–2008
programs for CCCC feature as many (i.e., as few) presentations on reading pedagogy as they do on grammar instruction,
a subject our discourse generally regards as only tangentially
important to the teaching of writing. Mariolina Salvatori and
Patricia Donahue (2012) investigated the lack of reading the-
ory/pedagogy panels at CCCC and found that reading disappeared for 17 years from the categories of interest on CCCC
proposals. Salvatori and Donahue celebrate the 2008 return
of reading as a category, but they are also troubled by the long
disappearance: "Although it is encouraging (and downright
exciting) to see that since 2008, the words *theories*, *reading*, and
writing appear in association, it remains puzzling that for seventeen years the word *reading* was completely invisible. A hiatus
of seventeen years?" (210). Reading's absence as a category, of
course, does not mean reading was completely absent from the
conference. To present their work over the years, Salvatori and
Donahue found ways to "work around, manipulate, or 'psych
out' the areas of interest legitimized by the CFP form" (211).
Even though reading may not have been completely removed
from CCCC for those years, it was less visible as a topic that mattered to the field: "Why should one engage in inquiry that has
been waved to the disciplinary borderlands or erased from the
map altogether?" (210).[3]

Although some graduate programs embrace reading pedagogy and theory, it is probably safe to say that most graduate
courses do not address the subject in much detail. Reflecting
on the difficulty of effectively incorporating reading pedagogy into graduate teacher training, Linda Adler-Kassner and
Heidi Estrem (2007) note a lack of resources: "at the same
time as instructors ask for more explicit guidance with reading pedagogy, that pedagogy is rarely included in composition
research, graduate composition courses, or first-year writing

program development materials" (36). If reading is absent from the books, articles, and conference presentations that shape our current conversations and influence the next group of teacher-scholars, then the teaching practices brought into the classroom will most likely consist of a hodgepodge of (perhaps unconscious and thus unexamined) reading strategies and theories. What most likely does not happen is any explicit theorization of how reading can be learned, taught, and connected with writing.

Most of the scholarship on reading is found in the field of education, which creates the impression that reading is something to be taught and learned by high school, and in the field of psychology, which can reinforce assumptions about reading being only a decontextualized act of decoding. As Marguerite Helmers (2003) points out, "Reading research, largely empirical in nature, has taken place under the auspices of the International Reading Association (IRA), an organization to which most college professors in English do not belong" (4). Another sign of how college composition has become distanced from reading pedagogy can be seen in academic journals. With the rise of the sociocultural definition of literacy, many academic journals dropped the word *reading* from their titles and replaced it with *literacy* (Lankshear and Knobel 2003), and those that remained journals about reading are largely concerned with literature or secondary education. While these title changes are understandable, they indicate and reinforce the perception that reading pedagogy in college is remedial. Many postsecondary compositionists are engaged in *literacy* research and contribute to *literacy* journals, but few would be described as contributing to *reading* scholarship, a situation unlikely to spur more reading research in composition. What has occurred, then, is a recursive situation in which the assumption that "students should already know how to read" feeds into the conception that reading pedagogy is not a high-status, worthwhile area of scholarship in the university, which continues to obscure a more complex view of reading inside and outside the classroom.

With the proliferation of reading anthologies for first-year composition, some might argue that we do attend to reading pedagogy. As teachers cram in readings and use less than half of an anthology, they may feel they've devoted more than enough time to reading. In my experience, and from conversations with colleagues and teachers at conferences, the introductory how-to-read material in anthologies may get *assigned* but not *taught.* Of course, handbooks and anthologies can only reveal so much about what actually happens with reading in the composition classroom. Yet without recent research, it's difficult to determine what teachers are actually doing with reading, and I take this scholarly absence as more evidence of reading's absence from composition's theoretical and pedagogical concerns.

Two brief examples, however, are probably accurate in their descriptions of teachers' difficulties with reading pedagogy. In Lisa Bosley's (2008) study of seven English teachers at a large southeastern university, she noted "faculty members viewed reading as discovering authorial intent rather than as a developmental, active process of constructing meaning" (290). They also were not "confident of their ability to define the complex process of critical reading, or to teach students how to do it well" (298). As Writing Program Administrators, Linda Adler-Kassner and Heidi Estrem (2007) have seen similar teaching problems with new graduate teachers. Despite the preparation for reading pedagogy offered in the composition practicum, Adler-Kassner and Estrem note they "have seen many new graduate instructors fall back into a way of teaching that constructs students as passive readers" (39). Based on the graduate teachers' difficulties with teaching reading, Adler-Kassner and Estrem realized they needed to devote more time to reading pedagogy in the practicum. I don't want to generalize these accounts to all programs and all teachers, but I suspect they may be indicative of widespread gaps and inconsistencies in the teaching of reading. The teachers in Bosley's study lacked confidence in their ability to teach reading, and they "expressed the desire to teach reading more effectively and explicitly" (298). I imagine many composition teachers feel the same way, and the feeling must be compounded as different genres and media accumulate, offering more challenges to already under-theorized reading pedagogies.

HOW READING DISAPPEARED

Composition's strongest period of reading research was during the 1980s and early 1990s. In their description of this period, Mariolina Salvatori and Patricia Donahue (2012) credit reader-response theories for positioning "readers at the center of the interpretive enterprise." By putting readers at the center of interpretation, theorists moved their focus "from what texts mean to how readers make them mean" (202). When writing teachers viewed students as actively constructing texts through both reading and writing, "a door was opened. Once opened, that door made the study of students as readers, the reading activities of students in the writing classroom, and how those activities would shape and affect their writing, a theoretical and ethical must" (203). Salvatori and Donahue's enthusiasm for this period is clear in their narration of events. Teacher-scholars were developing reading pedagogy, investigating connections between reading and writing, and trying to understand how students interpreted texts (Bartholomae and Petrosky 1986; Berthoff 1981; Donahue and Quandahl 1989; Flower 1988; Hull and Rose 1990; Salvatori, 1983).

In "The Reception of Reader-Response Theory," Patricia Harkin (2005) provides an interesting account of how reader-response theory became an accepted and invisible practice in literary studies, and how its place in composition studies was prominent until professionalization led to a focus on writing over reading. Harkin's account is driven by a nostalgia for the excitement reader-response theory generated, reminding us that "the theory boom took the power of meaning making away from the author (exclusively), but only reader-response gave that power to any old reader. At its most radical, for instance in the work of Bleich and Holland, reader-response offered no principle for ruling any reading *out*" (416, italics original). The power of the author was being overturned in the literature classroom. However, in the composition classroom, the goal was often to celebrate the power of the individual writer. The student author was no longer in need of simple grammar training—he was inventing the university, appropriating unfortunate "Engfish," and writing without teachers (Bartholomae 1985; Elbow 1973; Macrorie 1970). Teaching reading, the consumption of texts, would have seemed like a step backward given this momentum. Also, acknowledging the authority of readers in a writing classroom might subvert the authority teachers wanted to encourage in student writers, many of whom lacked confidence in their abilities. As Harkin (2005) notes, some of composition's reluctance to pursue reading as a subject for research and pedagogy grew out of its desire to distinguish itself as a field: "But just as literary theorists strove not to be tainted by composition, it's fair to say that composition studies ultimately saw itself as tainted by reader-response—indeed by all literary theory. What may have begun simply as an effort to shake free from literary studies had the not-always-intended effect of excluding all instruction in reading" (421).

Salvatori and Donahue (2012) argue that this disciplinary rift was both cause and effect of the "confusion about reading so prevalent in English studies—confusion related, in part, to conflicting and problematic claims about disciplinary ownership, about 'who' can be said to own 'what.' Does composition 'own' writing? Does literature 'own' reading?" (201). In their view, the confusion regarding ownership has repeatedly overshadowed an integrated view of reading and writing: "the problem of ownership has been variously inscribed and reinscribed in the narratives of English studies, continuously truncating or bypassing the nexus between reading and writing, only to confront and cross it again, at crucial moments of self-definition [for the disciplines]" (201). Although the question of ownership gets raised in the scholarship of the 1980s and 1990s, a more vital issue being investigated was the nexus between reading and writing. Some regarded that nexus, that connection, as a way to unite the divided disciplines and create more comprehensive meaning-making practices in the classroom.

Anthony Petrosky's (1982) essay "From Story to Essay: Reading and Writing" is an important piece of scholarship from that period because of how it outlines the problem of and offers a solution to the reading-writing division—a division that would shift in various ways but largely remain in composition for the next 30 years. He argues that rigid disciplinary boundaries have led to a situation in which "work in reading, response to literature, and composition has gone on independently" (19). Petrosky's concern is that teachers and students will practice and experience a simplified version of human understanding: "Reading, responding, and composing are aspects of understanding, and theories that attempt to account for them outside of their interactions with each other run the serious risk of building reductive models of human understanding" (20). In the essay, Petrosky reviews scholarship on reading and connects that scholarship to the work of literary theorists Louise Rosenblatt, Norman Holland, and David Bleich. He illustrates how "these three theorists are, basically, making the same claims about reading as the reading people" (20). Petrosky's essay was among a cluster of essays in an issue of *College Composition and Communication* that devoted half its space to the topic of reading-writing connections. (Bruce Petersen [1982] would publish work similar to Petrosky's later that same year in *College English*.) The work Petrosky does in the essay—synthesizing insights from reading, composition, and literary theory—pointed composition in a direction that was largely abandoned.

Deeper investigation into the nexus between reading and writing was instead replaced by an oversimplified view that acts of reading and writing are interrelated to the degree that specialized, different pedagogical approaches are unnecessary. That is, even if teachers are not explicitly teaching reading, students will learn about reading through its natural connection to writing. The "commonsense appeal" of this view of reading-writing "seemed to block rather than stimulate the production of new ideas about how to teach reading, writing, and their interanimation" (Salvatori and Donahue 2012, 205). The direction not taken—the one that blocked new ideas about reading-writing connections—can be seen in a discussion by Erika Lindemann (1993) and Gary Tate (1993) in *College English*. At the heart of the discussion was the purpose of first-year composition, and the relationship of reading to writing was a central question. An interesting and telling feature of the discussion was how reading was equated with literature, and how that equation determined how texts would be taught and read. Lindemann (1993) argued against incorporating literature into composition classrooms because literature would place the "focus on consuming texts, not producing them" (313). If "reading" meant "reading litera- ture," then reading was an obstacle to the goals of the writing classroom. If writing and the production of texts were opposed to literature and the consumption of texts, then writing had to be opposed to reading. Marguerite Helmers (2003) comments on the enduring frame of the discussion: "the debate defined the terms that were to endure: literature and writing, not read- ing and writing" (8). Out of all of the conflicts in the profession of English, Peter Elbow (1993) regarded this split as a "war," as "the most striking and problematic conflict of all: that between reading and writing—between literature and composition" (5). The foundational conflation of "reading" and "literature" and all of the pedagogical, theoretical, and disciplinary baggage associated with the literature/composition divide has resulted in wariness toward spending too much class time on theorizing and teaching reading. Therefore, resistance to reading peda- gogy in composition remains today, and much of that resistance is rooted in how we define ourselves and each other in compo- sition and literature, as we rely on binary oppositions in order to distinguish ourselves as a discipline. These binaries result in often-unconscious associations (reading is consumption; writ- ing is production) that oversimplify what we know to be com- plex literacy acts.

The desire to professionalize and distinguish composition from literature, then, is one major reason behind the absence of reading pedagogy. However, the reading-writing split was not purely due to divisions between composition and literature. Another strong influence upon that 1980s period of reading-writing scholarship was cognitive psychology. According to Judith Langer and Sheila Flihan (2000), investigation into the relationships between reading and writing was motivated by the "extensive research on cognitive processes in the separate fields of writing and reading, primarily from a constructivist perspective" (112). The shift in psychology from behaviorist perspectives to constructivism led to two important tools, cognitive process models and protocol analysis (think-aloud protocols). When applied to reading and writing, these tools helped replace the conception of a linear writing process with recursive, dynamic models of how writers plan, evaluate, and revise.

Typically associated with the work of Linda Flower and John Hayes (1981), cognitive approaches to composition also considered how reading and writing interacted. Such approaches to studying reading and writing would attempt to merge cognitive and social factors, but the "cognitive vs. social" views of research and pedagogy became something of another divide in the 1990s: "Although many composition theorists agree that both the social and the cognitive must be considered *in theory*, when it comes to pragmatic discussions about what should actually be taught in the classroom, the supposed agreement breaks down" (Foertsch 1995, 363, italics original). The social turn in literacy studies and composition studies at this time inspired research that investigated reading and writing as acts situated in specific social contexts; this turn helped make cognitive approaches seem asocial and too focused on a decontextualized mind—and less appealing as methods (Anson and Schwegler 2012, 162; Yagelski 2000, 61).[4] Reflecting on this loss, which he blames on "faddishness" and a "kind of collective attention deficit," John Hayes (2001) argues for multiple research methods that include cognitive studies and social theories (184). As Hayes rightly states, no theory can account for complex reading and writing acts without attending to "an appropriate combination of cognitive, affective, social, and physical conditions" (176). Unfortunately, cutting ties with educational and psychological research seems to be another way in which composition chose to professionalize and distinguish itself.[5]

Mariolina Salvatori (1996) points to a crucial issue of reading-writing pedagogy that has been lost among these disciplinary shifts: the issue "is not merely the question of whether reading should or should not be used in the composition classroom. The issue is *what kind of reading* gets to be theorized and practiced" (443, italics original). This is a question that has been unexplored in recent years by composition scholars. But it is a question all teacher-scholars should attend to because we are always teaching our students how to read: "The different ways students are asked to read imply particular values and beliefs about the nature of texts, the nature of readers as subjects of texts and as subjects in the world, and about meaning and language itself" (McCormick 1994, 7). That is, if we assign texts without teaching how they can or are expected to be read, then that implies a certain relationship between readers and texts and contexts; it implies the context is neutral, that the reader and text do not change for that specific situation; it implies readers do not have to strategically alter how they approach a text in a given context. An effective reading pedagogy does more than supply a few reading strategies at the front of an anthology. A theory and pedagogy of reading puts forth a view of readers, texts, and contexts: What does it mean to be a reader today? What should count as a text? What is the reader's relationship to the text and context? How is a reader constructed by the situation and previous reading experiences?

Teachers who think the introductory writing course is already filled with too many demands might resist such questions. However, I do not think students can learn critical literacy practices without considering these questions. Furthermore, the problems posed by the lack of an adequate reading pedagogy are compounded by the range of reading practices taking shape with new media. As literacy takes on more forms and purposes, students are expected to engage in reading/writing practices across a wider array of literacy sites, to negotiate ever-increasing amounts of information, to differentiate among sources of varying quality. In establishing a pedagogy that meets the challenges of contemporary literacy, composition needs to regard, study, and teach reading and writing as interrelated acts of literacy. A more robust reading pedagogy would not only address the questions described above, but it would also consider how to help students learn and use more dexterous, flexible reading strategies that stress adaptability in a time of fast literacy change.

Without a robust reading pedagogy we will struggle to help students critically navigate the resources made available by new media, even as we ask them to compose in new media. In order to begin to develop an effective reading pedagogy, we need first to examine students' existing strategies for reading across old and new media. Without studying and understanding students' reading practices in the various genres and media available through technology, we lack a complex view of student literacy. We may incorporate the writing of various genres into the classroom, but how do students interpret those genres as readers, and how do they envision their writing being read? We may try to incorporate digital genres and media into our classrooms, but how might conflicts arise from the different values students attribute to them at home and at school? A complex view of literacy—of both writing and reading, and the interactions between the two—takes such questions into account.

EXPANDING READING AND WRITING

The concept of literacy has expanded. Literacy in the singular form previously denoted a set of skills that led to social and cognitive development. This singular form embodied the view that literacy was autonomous, operating on its own, not influenced by social situations or shaped by powerful institutions. Literacy, as a set of decoding skills, could be mastered and measured. As historical and anthropological scholarship questioned this singular form of literacy and its supposed effects, the conception of literacy changed, with literacy viewed as taking on multiple forms and shaped by social, cultural, economic, and political forces (Graff 1987; Lankshear and Knobel 2003; Street 1995). With this new understanding, literacies include diversity of language and culture as well as the range of expressive

modes offered by various media. Instead of literacy being tied
to alphabetic text and a set of encoding-decoding skills, literacy
is recognized in a range of semiotic modes and in the various
life domains of schools, homes, workplaces, and public spaces,
where literacies are valued and used in different ways (Barton
and Hamilton 1998).

In one of her many contributions to this expanded sense
of literacy, Deborah Brandt (1995) offers an alternative to the
perceived challenges of the "rising standard of basic literacy,"
which instead "may be more usefully regarded as the effects
of a rapid proliferation and diversification of literacy" (651).
That is, instead of regarding a singular, "basic literacy" as the
measure of literacy challenge and achievement, it is the ability to adapt to multiple literacies that measures literate ability.
Through Brandt's interviews that detail twentieth-century literacy changes, she depicts literacy as "accumulating," with this
accumulation "developing in two directions—vertically (a piling up) and horizontally (a spreading out)" (652). One form of
"piling up" involves how "materials and practices" from old and
new forms of literacy coexist in society and "within the experiences of individuals." At any particular site of literacy—home,
school, or workplace—the practices and materials of old and
new literacies may be present. As Brandt observes, accumulation leads to "a piling up of literate artifacts and signifying practices that haunt the sites of literacy learning" (665).

In the horizontal sense, Brandt notes "literacy has literally
spread out across the century, reorganizing an array of economic, legal, political, and domestic activities" (652). As literacy
reorganized this array of activities it became linked to how one
successfully engages in those activities. If a particular form of
literacy spreads out and becomes more integrated into various
domains, it may rise in prominence as another form fades. In
many domains, for instance, e-mail is a more prominent, useful
form of communication than physical mail, which has largely
faded. Literacy has circulated through various life domains and
piled up within them. Consequently, Brandt argues, being literate now means having to "piece together reading and writing

experiences from more and more spheres, creating new and hybrid forms of literacy where once there might have been fewer and more circumscribed forms" (651). Within and across life domains literacy users draw materials and practices from the piles of literacy to which they have access.

This accumulation of literacy is not without conflict. To function well in particular situations, people must have access to and experience with the "right" kinds of literacy. In college, for instance, students less familiar with the expectations and moves of academic writing will have more adjustments to make than those who can more easily draw from the academic literacy practices in their accumulated experience. Literacies are also, in a sense, in competition with each other. Piling up and spreading throughout history, culture, and individual lives, literacies become imbued with a mixture of values and uses. These values and uses vary and clash in different settings and different times. When new literacies spread into more domains and push traditional literacies to the margins, the values, uses, and continued existence of those traditional literacies can be called into crisis. The "death of the book," the decline of handwritten letters, and national surveys that report on decreased reading are but a few obvious examples of such crises.[6] Values are at the heart of the crisis rhetoric, expressed through concerns that the culture is losing traditional forms of learning and expression. Alternatively, some sites of literacy may value and use traditional literacies to the extent that they attempt to block new literacies from spreading into their spaces. To continue Brandt's visual model for accumulation, imagine literacies jostling into each other as they rise up and circulate. The literacies chosen and used by individuals, groups, and institutions signal to themselves and to others what they (appear to) value. When those values conflict, so do literacies.

Some of the conflict accompanying accumulation is evident in the composition classroom. As noted earlier in this chapter, composition has expanded its sense of writing, incorporating more of the accumulating genres and media into its pedagogy and research. The expansion has raised questions about how we define writing and ourselves as a field. Kathleen Yancey (2004) notes literacy has experienced "tectonic change" in recent years through technological changes (298), with the reverberations leading to questions about composition's relevance and purposes: What counts as writing? How can teachers of writing stay relevant when so much writing occurs outside of school, and it looks so different from what we teach? In response to these changes and questions, she offers a curriculum that engages multiple modalities and audiences. The ambitious, expanded curriculum, she observes, would also require a concerted effort to create more courses and a major in composition (315). Even with a full vertical curriculum, developing courses in composition requires making choices among competing literacies and the values associated with them.

Don Kraemer (2007) considers the ethical implications of our choices as teachers in his reflection on the persistent and important question "What is college level writing?" Composition classes have only so much time, and teachers must make choices regarding what to include and what to leave out: "Which books to use and what kinds, what kinds of writing to assign and how much—these are ethical questions because every text we assign is a choice imposed on students, a choice made by teachers committing students to something rather than something else" (97). The choices imposed on students may benefit some over others. Turning toward his own curricular choices and values, Kraemer admits that his curriculum

> limits the choices of students who might prefer learning strategies to write more expressively, of students who would rather find information they can spread, of students who desire a non-rhetorical focus on correctness, of students who want to read something by non-whites, non-males, non-academics. Even more generally, this curriculum puts at a disadvantage students who wish to be rewarded for strengths that are not explicitly asked for by assignments such as mine. (109)

Kraemer's considerations are worth quoting because, on the surface, they seem obvious: a curriculum is always a set of values, choices, and effects. However, I think his comments articulate the detail and depth of the ethical aspects of our choices that may not rise to the forefront of our thinking as we put together classes semester after semester. This ethical discussion of curricular values and choices becomes even more urgent when put in perspective with literacy accumulation (and acceleration, as I'll argue in chapter three). As digital literacies jostle for curricular space with traditional literacies in the composition classroom, we continue to ask: Which literacies do we choose, and who benefits from those choices?

As this chapter has shown, composition has made choices about literacy that reflect a perception that reading and writing compete (for classroom time, for priority given to students as readers versus as writers), and that competition has manifested in conflicts over the values assigned to the teaching of particular literacy practices. Literacy competition and conflict can also be seen in questions over the role of new communication technologies and "old" alphabetic essay writing in curricula. These two literacy conflicts have shaped composition research and pedagogy in recent decades. Although each arose out of a different context, at this disciplinary and technological moment the two conflicts are related. The potential for user-generated content offered by Web 2.0 connects reading and writing more intimately than ever before, while the expansion of composition research and pedagogy into digital composing without a complementary exploration of contemporary reading practices would result in a significant gap in our literacy scholarship and teaching. Reading and writing need to be understood as literacy counterparts; we cannot fully understand one without the other. In order to reunite reading and writing in composition research and pedagogy, we first need to ask, what does it mean to be a reader in the twenty-first century? The remainder of this book seeks to answer that question.

NOTES

1   In "Using Reading in the Writing Classroom," Donna Qualley (1993) describes how she assigns double-entry journals, informal reading responses, and "reader-based" essays to foster a reading-writing interaction that

leaves a prominent trace of students' reading experiences. I realize that some teachers assign variations on reading responses and journals, but I wonder how common these assignments are and how much time teachers spend responding to such assignments. Reading can also leave a trace in the use of sources, but how much time do teachers have to respond deeply to the reading involved in source use, rather than primarily to writing aspects such as the integration of quotations? Time is always a significant issue in a writing course, but it becomes even more limited as curricula respond to literacy accumulation by incorporating more forms of reading and writing.

2   At times, it may sound as though I am slipping into an autonomous view of reading when I discuss how to improve students' reading or to make them "better readers." But what I typically mean by "better" involves a meta-awareness of reading as a strategic, situated process (Goggin 2008; Selber 2004).

3   As I have presented on and written about this topic I encountered some skeptical questions: What about graduate programs that do focus on reading pedagogy? What about CCCC panels that did not include the word *reading* in the title but that nevertheless addressed the subject? What about the large number of textbooks that include instructional material on reading? Of course, some graduate programs do attend to reading pedagogy. (Indeed, I know of some that do this well.) As Salvatori and Donahue (2012) stipulate in a footnote, the topic of reading "might have appeared under a variety of guises, on different panels, in different sessions" (215). However, as someone who has been actively searching for such presentations over the years, I must say that if many existed, they were not easy to find. And, even though textbooks may provide solid teaching suggestions, I do not think textbooks can provide teachers what they need: a sustained and complex theory and pedagogy of reading.

4   Robert Yagelski (2000) notes a "puzzling sort of paradox" that came with the social turn. Cognitive research on the writing processes of individuals "came to be viewed by many as too narrowly focused on the individual writer and was critiqued as generalizing the cognitive aspects of writing in ways that ignored the broader social and cultural contexts of writing as well as the inherently political nature of literacy." Yet, this broader view of the individual, he suggests, has sometimes lost a sense of the individual writer: "In short, as we began to understand individual writers and readers as manifestations of complex social and cultural factors relating to race, class, and gender, and to see their writing and reading as always situated within social and cultural contexts, we often seemed to ignore the specificity of the literate acts that those individual writers engage in; as we explore the inherently social and cultural nature of the individual, we seem to ignore the inherently individual nature of writing and reading" (61).

5   Composition theory and research is not alone in its struggle to find a satisfactory view of the relationship between the social and the cognitive.

In "Epistemological Tensions in Reading Research and a Vision for the Future," Victoria Purcell-Gates (2012) notes reading research is still in need of a sociocognitive frame that can unite its strands of research that tend to focus on one or the other. She suggests a wider research lens that can view both the cognitive and the social, with the "cognitive nested within sociocultural contexts" (469).

6   In 2009 the National Endowment for the Arts (NEA) released *Reading on the Rise*, a report on national reading data. As the title states, reading increased across nearly every demographic. Two things are interesting about the report. First, the survey incorporated online reading much more clearly than previous NEA surveys, which suggested digital media as a cause for reported declines in reading. Second, although online reading correlated highly with print reading, NEA Chair Dana Gioia still presented them in conflict as he reflected on reading's decline in previous surveys: "A decline in both reading and reading ability was clearly documented in the first generation of teenagers and young adults raised in a society full of videogames, cell phones, iPods, laptops, and other electronic devices" (NEA 2009, 2). Even when online and print reading are connected in a reading increase, the crisis narrative that pits digital reading against print reading will not allow it.

2

PERCEPTIONS OF LITERACY

*"How is it that what we teach [. . .] can be so different from
what our students know as writing?"*
—Kathleen Yancey (2004, 298)

Composition prides itself on being student-centered. Much of
our rhetoric and our practice focuses on "meeting students
where they are," keeping up with changes occurring in literacy
practices outside of formal education, and including students'
literacies in our classrooms to create a more interactive, hybrid
learning space. The accumulation of literacies, particularly literacies associated with communication technologies, has given
teachers more opportunities to meet students where they are, to
tap into the experiences and interests of students. In the past,
this meant classrooms engaged in hypertext, e-mail, and MUDs
(multi-user domains). More recently, classrooms have shifted to
include assignments involving blogs, wikis, Facebook, Twitter,
videos, and podcasts.[1] We have pursued these developments for
many reasons, most involving variations on the need to stay relevant and shape students' use of literacies in and out of school.
Another reason, which may drive our classroom efforts at chasing ever-newer forms of literacy more than we realize, is that we
want students to enjoy writing. We envy the pleasure and ease
with which students write beyond our doors. Reflecting on all of
the writing occurring beyond school, Kathleen Yancey suggests
what is lacking from composition classrooms: "Note that no one
is *making* anyone *do* any of this [out-of-school] writing. Don't
you wish that the energy and motivation that students bring
to some of these other genres they would bring to our assignments? How is it that what we teach and what we test can be so
different from what our students know as writing?" (298, italics

DOI: 10.7330/9780874219333.c002

original). At least in part, we hope that bringing in genres and media from the outside will also bring some of that enthusiasm and motivation that drive out-of-school writing.

Of course, bringing these genres and media into the class-room is not without complication. One source of complication is the paradox of literacy accumulation: although more litera-cies give us more inroads to "meet students," they also create more pressure for teachers to keep up with these developments. That challenge to keep up can be not only intimidating, but also overwhelming when unequal access to resources means some teachers will face material and other constraints that may delay or prevent their becoming familiar with and adopting new lit-eracy practices in the classroom. Also, the perceptions we have of students' digital literacy practices are not always accurate, which means we sometimes ask students to engage at a level of familiarity or proficiency beyond them. Even when students are familiar and proficient, the educational context creates expecta-tions and perceptions in their minds that can block the transfer of out-of-school practices to classroom literacy situations (see chapter five).

This chapter examines perceptions of literacy. The beliefs teachers have about literacy, about how it exists beyond the classroom, and how it may be enacted by students in class— these shape writing pedagogy. Similarly, students' beliefs about literacy influence what they count as reading and writing and how they see themselves as readers and writers.[2] Perceptions of literacy significantly shape the reading and writing practices in which people engage. In their theorization of literacy as a social practice, David Barton and Mary Hamilton (1998) state, "In the simplest sense literacy practices are what people do with liter-acy. [. . .] This includes people's awareness of literacy, construc-tions of literacy and discourses of literacy, how people talk about and make sense of literacy" (6). Perceptions of literacy are not merely tied to but bound up in and flow through how we see ourselves, how we relate to other people, and how we under-stand what counts as literacy. These perceptions are tied to iden-tity and how we act as users of literacy. Connections between literacy and identity are complex and fraught with issues of power, as demonstrated by ethnographies of literacy (Barton and Hamilton 1998; Heath 1983; Street 1995). As Bronwyn Williams (2009) states, "Rather than reveal a single authentic 'self,' such research has emphasized that our performances of identity through literacy may be shifting and are always contingent on the cultural context" (93). Literacy changes in different contexts, taking on other shapes and purposes. A way to understand this changing shape is to divide cultural contexts into different life domains, such as home, school, and work. Within these domains, social institutions such as family and education have explicit and implicit methods—rules, penalties, social conventions—for supporting particular kinds of literacies. The different social relationships, resources, values, and rules that surround literate activity in these domains give literacies different patterns and structures. Domains have boundaries, but those boundaries are also porous, with "leakages and movement between boundaries, and [. . .] overlap between domains" (Barton and Hamilton 1998, 9–10). At home, certain literacies may be valued that are different from those at school or at work. The more these literacies diverge in a given context, the more tension there is for those negotiating the identity shifts. The identity work accompanying the learning of reading and writing, then, is never simple.

This chapter digs into that identity work, exploring who the case study participants are as readers at school and at home. What do they read? How do they read? How do they perceive reading and themselves as readers? Justifiably, educators wonder about the literacy influences students bring into the classroom from home and the web. However, this study's participants' comments demonstrate that sometimes we underestimate how perceptions of "valuable" and "worthwhile" literacy— often associated with real or imagined educational priorities— can influence readers and writers beyond school. This observation raises questions about the role of educational institutions in popular perceptions of literacy: What messages are sent out from school that shape perceptions of literacy? What values are being reinforced or undermined? Education is a powerful institution that largely supports dominant literacy practices associated with objective, consumable, testable, print-based content. Barton and Hamilton (1998) observe that the "vernacular literacies which exist in people's everyday lives are less visible and less supported" than dominant literacies (10). Although teachers of traditional literacy may feel under siege by new technologies and the pop culture messages that reinforce them, they probably underestimate the power of dominant literacies and the cultural messages that exist about them. As this chapter illustrates, participants have internalized the "pedagogization of literacy" (Street and Street 1995) and cultural narratives that reinforce a relatively narrow view of reading and writing.

THE PARTICIPANTS

The nine student participants attended Midwest High School, a school with a population of nearly 1,700 students located in an urban area. It is an excellent school, but its excellence is also complicated. Over 90 percent of its graduates go on to post-secondary education. On state and national tests it meets and exceeds standards. The school is diverse in terms of race and gender, but not as much in economic status. The low number of students eligible for food stamps has prevented funding for remedial education and courses; as a result, some students flounder compared to the better-prepared students. During my visits to the school I was impressed by the enthusiasm in the hallways and in the classrooms. As the teachers concurred, Midwest has motivated, energetic students who genuinely appreciate their school. Such qualities make teaching somewhat easier, but much of the teaching for such an excellent school is based around tests and a top-down model of learning. The school's above-average standing was the primary reason for studying its students: How do "good readers" read in and out of school?

Mark, James, Nadia, Sarah, Lauren, Amy, David, Tim, and Diana are the student participants. I also interviewed and observed Julia, an English teacher with over twenty years of experience. In addition, interviews with Angela, the head librarian, and four participants' families furthered my understandings of the school and the participants.

(For more information on the participants and my approach to this study, see the Appendix.)

LITERACY MYTHS AND SCHOOL DISCOURSES

I waited for Tim in the College and Career Center, a small room near the back of Midwest's library. Each participant scheduled for an interview had a note excusing the missed class period; sometimes I had to ask the librarian to call advising and remind the student about the interview. Waiting at the long conference table, I scanned the bookcases and shelves filled with college catalogs and brochures, test preparation books, financial aid books, and advertisements from local colleges and universities. One college advertisement featured a student, smiling and confident, holding a book and standing above a line of red, fiery text: "Ignition. Knowledge is the engine of success. Rev it up." The words leaned to the right, as if in motion, ready to blaze across the page. Other ads and brochures made similar statements, but in less colorful ways:

> "Your Education. Your Future."
> "College: Your Key to Success."
> "Knowledge. Career. Success."

In the large library space, metal shelving units stretched from the back wall and stopped short of several long tables near the front where students worked together or alone. One young woman read a newspaper alone at a table near two young men who flipped through a historical book about guns. Five students browsed the stacks. Along the far wall, opposite the entrance, students chatted with each other and typed at seven computer stations. Angela, director of the library, had bought furniture from yard sales with her own money and created a "living room" near the checkout desk, with comfortable chairs facing each other around a wood coffee table. The library was open to students throughout the day, even during lunch for those who wanted a quiet place to relax. Angela let the "living room" students be social, but she put on the appearance of enforcing typical library rules as she told the others to be quiet: "Ladies and gentlemen, you need to be working." As she returned to the desk, she told me, "I know they'll sit and talk with their books open, and I'm okay with that. But they have to keep the noise level down."

The library seemed progressive, providing spaces for students to socialize. I was also surprised to see unusual books in the stacks. A tall bookcase filled with graphic novels was stuck behind a column; it was out of the way—you would almost have to be a nosy researcher to notice it—but at least it existed and showed recognition of literacies beyond alphabetic text. I also noticed popular fiction by Dean Koontz, Stephen King, Robert Ludlum, Anne McCaffrey, and John Grisham on the literature shelves. I asked about these popular texts, and Angela replied, "That's been my doing. Anything to entice them to read. Not many students know about the graphic novels, but the few who do check out a lot of them."

As I headed back to the College and Career Center, I noticed "READ" posters plastered along the columns and walls. Actors, athletes, authors, and various other celebrities held books under the large, capitalized suggestion to "READ." One poster featured no celebrity, only the words "Read. Succeed." Other posters repeated similar statements about how reading leads to success. The posters in the library and the ad slogans in the College and Career Center reminded me of entrenched cultural narratives about literacy: the idea that reading equals literary reading, and what Linda Adler-Kassner and Susanmarie Harrington (2002) have called the "school-success narrative." The narrative was prominent in their analysis of public attitudes regarding literacy:

> At its heart is a familiar theme: A college education is the stepping-off point for entrance into middle-class society, and obtaining this education will ensure that students will participate in the perpetuation of that society and its values. A central requirement of getting this education is amassing and reproducing objective

literacy skills, which help to ensure that students are learning the appropriate material to facilitate participation in middle-class life. (62)

The school-success narrative contributes heavily to students' sense of their literate identity. Although they may not enjoy the means by which they have to achieve those "objective literacy skills," they tend to value and to cling to the narrative. The alternative of doubting the narrative would result in too much cognitive dissonance for most students, especially those already in or close to the middle-class lifestyle.

As I prepared for the interviews, I kept in mind the setting, my role as a college teacher, and the nature of the questions, which were about reading, writing, high school, and college/career plans. I expected and heard the entrenched cultural narratives about literacy. I did not mind that the educational setting probably directed their responses to a degree. Because I was ultimately interested in how and why reading takes the shape it does in college, it made sense to assume that the identity shifts the participants would perform in these interviews would be similar to the ones they would perform as students in a college classroom. That is, if they inflated their admiration of Shakespeare or downplayed their love of video games, then that would echo how most students typically behaved during the first few weeks in my classes. As expected, over time the participants did adjust some of their responses, which will be seen in chapter three.

I want to pause for a moment to reflect on the care I took interpreting interviews. Talking about literacy is not the same as doing things with literacy. That is, participants may describe complex literature as their favorite kind of reading, and they may only describe a few ways in which they read, but they could be exaggerating the former and unable to articulate the latter. To mitigate such possibilities, I interviewed the participants multiple times and gathered literacy histories (Barton and Hamilton 1998). I also wanted to see how their responses might change over time, which involved repeating questions about reading and writing. I interviewed and observed four of them at home. The nine students received e-mail follow-up questions. Also, interviews with Angela, the director of the library, Julia, a senior English teacher, and family members of four of the participants provided opportunities to check interpretations and gain fuller understandings of the participants. Finally, I viewed the interpretations against my experiences and knowledge as a teacher and scholar of literacy.

TYPES OF READING

When I asked, "Could you talk about your reading habits? What kinds of things do you read?" most students instantly responded by talking about literary fiction. A few said they did not read much, negatively identifying themselves with the statement "I'm not really a reader." I expanded the range of what "reading" meant in the interviews by asking about specific media and genres: magazines, biographies, websites, e-mail, instant messages, etc. Suddenly, the non-readers described a lot of reading. Even after I clarified what I meant by reading, most continued to equate reading with literature, often with recognizable classics. For instance, Mark consistently referred to particular works and authors as "having literary merit." These works and authors included the usual suspects: Shakespeare, Hemingway, Fitzgerald, Dickens, etc. Mark valued complex literature partially because it made him stand out—a kind of cultural capital—as someone who could read it: "I've always liked reading above my level, got a chip on my shoulder I guess, trying to prove that I can do that. So, I've always liked reading complex things, read stuff that maybe no one else is reading. Try to be different. I guess that's kind of dumb, but it got me reading."

As I reviewed the interview transcripts, I paid attention to how participants used value terms, comparisons, and binaries to represent themselves as readers. In the previous passage, Mark used the following language to describe reading: "above my level," "complex," "different." These phrases marked what counted as quality reading for many participants. When I asked about what he might do in the future, he said: "I want to teach.

I really like English. I'm really into Hemingway, because I know that's teachable. And I appreciate it when teachers display passion and respect for literature. That passion can inspire others to read these great things, the poems and stories and novels that do so much for people. I think teaching should do that for people and give passion to the things that should be read." For Mark, it seemed that one element of Hemingway's value was its place in school: it can be taught.

James made similar comments about literature's worth: "A big part of why I enjoy Poe and Shakespeare and others like them so much is because their writings have lasted so long and get studied so long. There's a greatness to them." Lauren and Diana echoed these statements, adding elements of the "school-success narrative." Listing a number of school-assigned authors, Lauren said, "If I can handle complex readings like the ones they've thrown at me, I'll do well in college and whatever reading I have to do for my job. Reading's so important to everything we do, and it can make a real difference in our lives." Diana expressed a similar sentiment:

> So many people can't read well. So many people waste time reading the wrong things. I know that makes me sound snobby, but my friends tried to get me to read *The Lovely Bones*, and I was, 'Oh, that's horrible. No way.' I like reading quality. I like being challenged, to keep my reading skills up because I know that will be important for the future. And I try not to read things that are too simple or easy. Too many people choose the simple path.

In these statements, Lauren and Diana expressed elements of autonomous literacy: "complex readings" will increase their general reading skills, allowing them to succeed with any kind of reading in the future. Diana's definition of worthwhile reading, however, is more interesting. She described *The Lovely Bones* as a "waste" of time and as one of "the wrong things" to read. It did not qualify as "quality" reading or as something that "challenged" Diana. Alice Sebold's novel was received well critically, and it isn't hard to think of other novels that would have been more deserving of Diana's criticism. In a later part of the interview, she repeated and emphasized how many of her friends

and family enjoyed the novel. Her dismissal of Sebold is com-
parable to how Mark valued reading that was "different" and
"above my level." That is, the popularity of the book devalued it
in her eyes. I think it is also interesting to note how her discussion of quality was tied to maintaining skills, a line of thought
that started with the observation that "many people can't read
well." In Linda Brodkey's "Tropics of Literacy," she argues that
literacy is used as a "social trope and the various definitions of
literacy as cultural Rorschachs" (Brodkey 1986, 47). The tropes
mark identity and difference, telling us "who we are by pointing out who we are not" (51). From the kinds of books people
put on shelves to the ways in which people read and write for
jobs, literacy places people socially, and people use literacy to
position themselves in relation to others. In many of these interviews, the participants seemed to define themselves as readers
of high culture instead of mass culture.

The high-low division of culture arose multiple times. Nadia
openly admitted her love of Fitzgerald and Hemingway, refer-
ring to their books as "classics" and saying, "No one writes like
them anymore. The language they used, the way they talked
about very human things, deep things—that's so rare." Nadia
seemed to value the difference between "high" and "low" literature, the enduring division between the classics and popular
literature. Later, Nadia laughed as she reluctantly admitted that
the *Harry Potter* books "are my favorite, even though they're not,
like, the best writing." She seemed embarrassed to admit that a
popular book meant so much to her. Articulate and poised most
of the time, Nadia stumbled through an explanation of *Harry
Potter*'s appeal:

> I'm not sure how to. . . . I feel dumb right now not having a great
> answer to that. I know and recognize that *Harry Potter* isn't the
> best literature ever. But I still like it. I don't know. I just—the
> friendships, I guess? I like the characters a lot. And it's so much
> fun watching them grow. And the stories are good, well told.
> It's . . . fun? I mean, those books are a lot of fun. They may not
> be the most difficult or literary things ever, but I do like reading
> them.

Nadia's hesitation to list "fun" as a reason for appreciating the books seems linked to the description that the novels do not exemplify "the best writing." Although she did not want to "bad mouth" the *Potter* series, Nadia said, "They're great to read, but just for simple enjoyment and pleasure." Although Nadia enjoyed reading some of the books assigned in school, the challenge of those books kept them hierarchically above books that provide "simple enjoyment."

Tim, David, Mark, and Amy all read graphic novels. They checked them out of the school library; David and Tim also collected graphic novels, buying them online and from local comic book stores. David was an avid reader of *Superman*, even collecting other comics that included him in crossover stories so he could "get the complete story." Mark, Tim, and Amy read manga, Japanese comics translated into English. Yet, none of the four participants considered graphic novels as a valid response to "What do you read?" When I asked them why, David gave a representative response: "I mean, I'll say 'I read comic books,' but it doesn't seem the same, like it qualifies as reading the way literature does. The art makes [the comics] seem like kid stuff." Amy said, "I hide the manga from my mom. She thinks they're stupid, and I just don't want to hear it. I think they're cool and interesting, even though I know they're mainly pictures." Holding up traditional literature as the standard for reading led to a devaluing of a literacy these participants actively pursued and enjoyed.

The visual aspect of graphic novels added to this devaluing. These four participants and I spoke at length about graphic novels after I made it clear that I read and enjoyed them. Although the participants expressed how much they liked reading in this genre, they still held a lower view of graphic novels. Mark was something of an exception. Part of Mark's explanation as to why he read comic books was the cultural value attached to reading "serious" and sophisticated kinds of comic books: "Manga's cool because I get to see Japanese culture and how they tell stories. Most of the manga I read have long, big stories—complicated stories. And I've read *Watchmen*, which is

American, and it is amazing how complicated it is. I'm not really into the simple comic books." Even when he admitted to reading comic books, he elevated "serious" kinds over others, which he regarded as "simple."

I had difficulty determining how students placed values on popular readings: some students easily admitted to reading popular texts, while others were more reluctant. The answer seems to involve the degree of popularity. As with most products in teen culture—music, television shows, movies—once books reach a tipping point in popularity and become widely read, their value decreases. Nadia's reluctance to declare her enjoyment of *Harry Potter* is one example. James, Mark, and Tim all described their "nerdy" enjoyment of thrillers and fantasy novels, downplaying the incredibly popular *Lord of the Rings*. Yet, they openly expressed their love of less popular books such as Stephen King's *Dark Tower* series. As James said, "I do like Tolkien's *Lord of the Rings*, but not nearly as much as other people. It's good, but I think King's [*Dark*] *Tower* has a lot more relevance and power." When Tim started talking about fantasy novels, he hesitated as he described his feelings for Tolkien's series in the statement "I like it okay." I reminded him to "speak freely and openly. Say whatever you want." Tim sounded more comfortable as he further described the series: "I love *Lord of the Rings*. Don't get me wrong. I'm convinced I'm a different person because of that book. But so many people like that and overlook *Dark Tower*, which is incredible and more mature in some aspects. I'm more open to—more likely to say I'm a *Tower* fan to others." The degree of popularity appears to matter. However, I think the explanation goes beyond teen culture and involves the long-standing view of "popular reading" as something simple that attracts unthinking audiences—an important point I will return to shortly.

Participants also minimized the time spent online. Diana said, "I don't like reading on the Internet, mainly because I think I'm a reading snob. Seriously, I feel like I'm reading below my level when I'm on. I'd much rather read a book or a magazine that's better written." When I asked her what she meant by "better written," she said: "So much of it [online writing] is short and simple. It doesn't feel like a challenge. And it's not like literature, with all these layers and complex symbolisms. I know magazines aren't literature or literary, but they at least give me news and the bigger picture of news and history. And I feel like I get more informed from that. News magazines aren't as easy as a lot of websites." Lauren read "tons of magazines"—print and online versions—but added, "I know I should expand beyond that. I just like getting all of those perspectives and information. But I don't spend a whole lot of time with the online ones. I just go and look for what I want."

When it came to MySpace or Facebook, participants admitted to using the sites, but with a reluctant tone. Sarah stated, "I know I shouldn't spend so much time on those places, and I kind of hate myself after it, but it's fun, and everyone else is on there. I mean, it's almost impossible not to [be on social sites]. If you aren't, then your friends complain about it. You might as well give in and avoid all the whining." They often pointed to friends for their use of such sites, which is a common claim found in other research (boyd 2008; Williams 2009). However, James was adamant in his lack of involvement: "I don't do MySpace or Facebook or blogs. It just doesn't interest me. When I go online it's to look something up. I want to go on and get it done." Whereas the other participants seemed embarrassed by their involvement with social networking sites, James appeared to take pleasure in expressing his disdain for them. When reviewing the audio recording, I was surprised by how emphatically James said, "I don't do MySpace or Facebook or blogs." It seemed important to him to convey how little regard he had for such reading and writing.

Part of the participants' reluctance in talking with me about their digital literacies probably came from not knowing how to talk to an educator about how they read digital media; they had no precedent for such matters being taken seriously in an educational context. Typically, when educators do bring texts perceived as "pop culture" into the classroom they do so with the goal of social critique or to protect students from being "duped" by consumer culture. Although I think the trend is shifting away from the culture-jamming perspective toward productive engagement with pop culture (Buckingham and Sefton-Green 1994; Jenkins 2008), it is doing so slowly. When Bronwyn Williams (2009) described to colleagues his research on how students use pop culture texts in their online literacy practices, he received responses of "disdain, alarm, or at best, discouragement" (187). For the students in his study, it was the first time an educator took them seriously in regard to these practices (24).

As a teacher who brings a wide range of media into every class, I regularly respond to students' surprise that the class will not only read and discuss digital genres, but write in them as well. At first, the reactions are a mix of curiosity, confusion, and unease. Some students welcome a change to typical class-room practices; however, those same students are often uneasy with the change because they are less familiar with the expec-tations for doing well. Others express confusion and discom-fort because the activities do not resemble school definitions of worthwhile reading and writing. As I justify and scaffold the assignments, these initial concerns are often assuaged. However, some of the original judgments remain. Based on these early interactions, and on feedback after the course is done, students sometimes regard such activities as a break—an interesting aberration—from typical coursework. These activi-ties "don't fit" into the expected vision of school. Although I carefully introduce this material with an explanation of clear educational objectives as well as purposes beyond the univer-sity's walls, the infrequency with which students engage in such practices for school appears to trump my efforts at making the endeavor seem more meaningful and useful. In a similar way, the participants' educational experiences cordoned off the def-inition of reading to include materials that resembled school literacy and shut out the rest.

The ideological force of educational literacy is not alone in shaping students' perceptions of literacy practices. Long-standing dismissals and fears of popular culture feed into and draw from this force. Sven Birkerts (1994), Mark Edmundson (2004), and Neil Postman (1986) are only a few of the many critics to assail pop culture's numbing influence upon the masses, who passively accept whatever flashes across the screen. Fingers point at pop culture's negative influence during times of social change (Littau 2006), especially when educational standards are seen to be in freefall. Edmundson, for instance, sees "little fire, little force of spirit or mind in evidence" in his students (10). He points to television and the World Wide Web as causes of his students' passive behavior in class:

> My students were the progeny of two hundred available cable channels and omnipresent Blockbuster outlets. They grew up with their noses pressed against the window of that second spectral world that spins parallel to our own, the World Wide Web. There they met life at second or third hand, peering eagerly, taking in the passing show, but staying remote, apparently untouched by it. (10)

Ironically, the opposite of the numb, passive student is also resisted by educational standards. If teachers were to assign *Harry Potter, Twilight,* or *Hunger Games*—three popular series that have attracted fervent fandom—they might be suspected of pandering to popular taste and giving in to easy pleasure instead of critical analysis.[3] Composition scholars T.R. Johnson (2003) and Laura Micciche (2007) have examined and argued against the view that pleasure and emotion run counter to serious, thoughtful engagement. Students have confidence and agency with the texts of digital media and popular culture in general, yet they adopt the dominant discourse regarding such texts—they are simple, frivolous, and probably bad for us. If there's a legacy of certain texts being seen as complex and deep while others are perceived as frivolous and shallow, then that will most likely affect how students situate themselves in relation to those texts. This kind of perception about what counts as reading—driven by binaries of high/low, simple/complex, and popular/classic—can help teachers understand how students make decisions about the reading strategies they adopt when they engage with texts.

WAYS OF READING

As students talked about the importance of reading certain texts and authors, they revealed their perceptions about good ways of reading, which meant deciphering symbols, comprehending themes, and understanding what the author meant. Arriving at the "correct" answer weighed heavily on the students' perceptions of school-based reading. Nadia said, "We did *Frankenstein* our first year, so I've been thrown in the deep end with complex stuff. If you work at it, you'll figure out what it means." Lauren similarly described reading as a way of solving a literary puzzle: "I love writing analysis papers in which I explain the author's symbolism. I don't know why, but I love figuring that stuff out." Every student repeated similar sentiments, from Mark saying, "I'm really good at reading and writing about symbolism now," to David's emphasis on the importance of vocabulary and key literary concepts, which helped him get through tests. Here again are echoes of what made reading worthwhile: "complex," "symbolism," and "deep end" denote difficult, not popular, material. When reading the interview transcripts for this section I paid attention to value terms, comparisons, and binaries; I was also interested in seeing descriptions of purposes and goals for reading.

A prominent goal of reading was to "figure out" the "correct" answer. Tim's teachers sometimes disagreed with his interpretations, which inspired him to find an unusual solution during his sophomore year: he avoided reading his sophomore assignments so he could read what his friends were assigned in the year ahead of him: "That year, I read *The Iliad*, *Macbeth*, and *Catcher in the Rye*. I heard my friends talking about how they didn't like or didn't understand them, and I wanted to see if my understanding was close to what the teacher told them." Tim read a year ahead in order to get the "answers" from his friends and to create a safe space for his interpretations.

When relating reading practices encouraged in other classes, students continually described the banking model of learning. Prominent phrases included "check knowledge" and "retain knowledge" and "just know it." James observed, "We might talk about the content of the readings in history class, but it's just to check events and knowledge. There's no discussion of the reading itself." When I asked James if "teachers ever talked about how to read textbooks," he gave me a blank look and shook his head. Mark's response to that question also signaled confusion: "They want us to read it, know it. Take it in. I think they [teachers] assume we can read it without much problem." David described the actions in a number of courses—psychology, humanities, government, and economics—as "mainly note-taking." He said the tests in his humanities course were "easy because I retained most of the information the teacher gave us in the note sessions." Sarah echoed the method of getting most of her information from in-class notes, adding that her "method for reading is pretty simple: go for the bold words. They're on the test. You don't really have to read—not all of it, I mean. And there's rarely a reason for the teacher to check you've read the whole thing."

At first, Amy did not know how to characterize the readings in her non-English classes. When I asked about class discussion, she replied, "We're just supposed to read it, get done with it, and do the lesson. We go through it pretty fast. We're not expected to sit around and talk about it. We're expected to know it." Although I did not visit classes outside of English, the descriptions of reading practices articulated by Amy and the other participants may have stemmed from a lack of overt instruction about reading strategies. The assignments and syllabi I examined from English classes gave no specific directions for reading, only indicating a reading had been assigned. Writing assignment sheets provided brief information about possible topics, but did not explicitly guide reading strategies. For instance, one assignment sheet gave students the option to "Write an essay analyzing the symbol of blood in *Macbeth.*" The implied reading strategy reinforced the style of reading for the deep, "hidden" meaning.

The participants readily spoke of writing processes and strategies, but they conveyed looks of confusion when asked about reading strategies. Even though a few students admitted to "not being very good at writing," they could still list different kinds of prewriting strategies, introduction options, organizational methods, and revision tips. They knew the five-paragraph format. They could even articulate how they had a metacognitive awareness of when writing was proceeding well or not. I asked, "Do you have any strategies for or awareness of your writing when it isn't going well, or do you see those things during revision?" Most of the students replied something similar to Amy's statement:

> Mostly as I'm writing. That's when I'll get a sense that a paragraph is full and has enough in it. I'll look back on the screen and see it, nice and thick. Or I'll know that a sentence "ran away from home"—that's what I call it when I just start rambling and have no idea how I got there. I'll look back and see where I was going and where I ended up. That's how I keep track as I go along. I'm sure I look back when I'm finished [writing], but most of the time I'm writing and then checking out what I did before going on.

Amy had conceptual language for when her writing went off topic. Amy's being able to formulate and apply a concept about writing suggests that she had more metacognitive awareness of her writing. Lauren talked about how her writing would "flow" and how she knew to look back at her writing later:

> When the writing is flowing, when it's just flowing out of me, I don't try to stop for a while. I go with it and get as much on screen as I can. Those flow moments aren't easy to find, so I don't let go of them. And then I look back over it and fix spelling and other stuff that went wrong along the way. Sometimes I'll spot words and things that don't belong and—out they go.

Sarah articulated how she calls early drafts "messy" instead of "rough":

> It's a thing I've been doing for years. I don't like to think of [early writing] as "rough." That means that all I need to do is make it less rough—fix this, fix that, make it smoother. But that's not how I write. It's messy, and you have to do more with a mess. You have to clean it up, move the mess [around], organize it, and throw stuff away and put other things where they should go. That makes so much more sense to me than "rough." Messes are messy. They take work.

Even if they did not always follow through on their vision of writing well, they had a framework and a language for working with writing. Only David and Tim talked about "winging it" with their writing and "not looking back or revising much." However, they were still aware of prewriting and revising strategies they could have used. As Tim said, "Yeah, I could revise. I'm really good at spelling and pretty good at grammar. I read a lot, so I have a good vocabulary. And [I know that] ideas shouldn't be thrown in randomly but put closer together. I could go back over it, but I don't." Amy's awareness of her writing is what teachers of reading want from students when reading: the ability to check for understanding, to make connections among ideas, to correct misunderstandings. Lauren was aware she should review her writing after producing large amounts of text. Sarah's articulation of an early draft as "messy" instead of "rough" signals a sophisticated view of writing.

Students had a much harder time, however, articulating reading strategies. Indeed, a few had fun with the perceived strangeness of the questions: "How do you read? Do you have strategies or an awareness of your reading—when it goes well, when it doesn't?" Sarah replied, "Well, I read one word and then the word after that, and if I'm feeling crazy, I'll read the word after that." James offered a representative response to the question about when reading doesn't go well: "If I don't get something, I just move on. If I don't get it, I'm probably not gonna get it." In terms of describing reading strategies, they could not go far beyond general statements of looking for symbolism and themes in English and looking for vocabulary, bold words, names, and dates in other classes.

Regarding literary reading, a significant factor that emerged in the interviews involved what counted as knowledge or a valid interpretation. Tim's comment was echoed by others: "Why reread it? If I get it wrong, I get it wrong. If I get it right, then that's that. I'll find out in class." Lauren said, "Other students are going to have their own opinions, and we all say stuff in class. The teacher ends up letting us know which one [interpretation] is the best." With comments like these, it became clear that several students believed the teacher possessed "the answer," and that their own interpretations would either be right or wrong. With a view like that, there's no point in returning to the text, gauging one's understanding, or considering other interpretations. Nadia talked about how to justify any interpretation:

> If you can justify your reading, then you can say just about anything. You can make the poem or whatever mean anything. So, just make it good. I'm usually really able to stand up for my views of the readings. And that's important, being able to do that—make an argument and stick to it. If others think I'm wrong, that's fine. But I know I have good reasons for my opinions.

Mark also spoke of justifying his interpretation: "The point is to justify it [your interpretation]. Do that, and you can say anything. I find the examples in the story that prove my view of it." It's unlikely that these viewpoints encouraged rereadings or attempts to check understanding along the way.

When Julia encouraged broader ways of reading from students they became frustrated. Julia was aware of reader-response theory and attempted to help students move beyond author-centered readings as well as solipsistic readings. She tried to push for analysis and an appreciation of difficulty, ambiguity, and multiple perspectives. As was evident during a classroom discussion on Bill Bryson's essay "The Future of English," her students had a hard time moving beyond their familiar modes of reading; much of the discussion revolved around students' lives or the exact words and thoughts of the author. Julia later noted how her students are often limited by looking for a conclusive answer:

> I want them to make a connection to their lives, but also to their social surroundings. When you read about nineteenth-century marriage, how does that reflect on how we view marriage today? And I find that my [Advanced Placement students] struggle with that. They keep trying to look at it formally, for the right way to look at it. That can be frustrating for them when we try to push beyond that. When so many other experiences—in school, outside school—habituate students to search for the answer, the right answer, then that's a tough situation to

work against when you want the class to have a different discussion, a different approach.

Angela, who taught students research in the library, echoed Julia's statements. Faced with multiple, high-stakes testing situations, students' reluctance to read in ways that cannot be easily assessed should not be surprising (Gallagher 2009). The participants' limited views of reading, in terms of what counts and how to do it, are not unique. According to the Pew Internet and American Life report *Writing, Technology and Teens*, respondents engaged in a wide range of writing practices. However, they defined writing in a narrow way, without including blogging, e-mail, texting, and other digital communications as writing (Lenhart et al. 2008). Joanne Addison and Sharon McGee (2010) point out, however, that composition instructors recognize these practices as forms of writing. Addison and McGee consider the Pew report in conjunction with their own research that suggests college students enjoy writing more than high school students do (and more than teachers would expect), and they point to a promising possibility: "Thus, teenagers may actually be writing more than ever but in a far greater variety of forms not normally recognized as part of the school or work experience. These results [. . .] do leave us with a positive note: for our students, writing is not necessarily the 'dreaded' activity that many of us imagine" (168). It is also evidence of the influence that educational and cultural definitions of literacy have on how people generally regard reading and writing. That is, the teens in the survey write blogs, but blogging cannot count as writing because it has been cordoned off with the other forms of pop culture writing, away from "legitimate" writing.

Brian Street and Joanna Street (1995) have named this phenomenon the "pedagogization of literacy," which spreads "at the expense of the many other uses and meanings of literacy evident from the comparative ethnographic literature" (106). Education's version of literacy, then, takes "on the character of an ideological force controlling social relations in general and conceptions of reading and writing in particular" (107). This force can alter how people give value, positive or negative, to particular literacies. This force can be so powerful as to make literate people feel illiterate. Jeanne Henry (2009) reflects on why both students and teachers should value a range of literacies, especially when students have less experience and confidence with dominant literacies: "I realized that if I took my students' everyday, vernacular literacies for granted, they probably did, too. Yet, these were literacy practices in which they not only engaged but also excelled" (66). Henry asked her students to examine their literacy practices and their attitudes about the practices, and she developed classroom activities to help them learn to value these everyday literacies: "I considered it progress to see the students begin to redefine themselves as people who liked to read some things, but not other things, because this made them like every other reader on the planet, rather than 'poor' or 'reluctant' readers" (67). Other attempts by teachers like Henry may help students value their own literacies. Without such interventions, though, it is likely that many people's views of their literacies will be shaped by the pedagogization of literacy.

Rebecca Rogers (2003) witnessed the effects of this ideological force when she examined the struggles a working-class woman and her daughter experienced with school discourse, which dominated over and devalued other literacies they possessed. Rogers notes the mother and daughter "were proficient with literacy and language and demonstrated considerable knowledge of institutional structures and social organizations" (156). Not only was this proficiency unable to help them overcome certain institutional and educational obstacles, but the experience also gave them "sets of assumptions about themselves in relation to this schooled literacy. That is, within this institutional context they have learned that they were not literate people" (152). The mother and daughter devalued their home literacy practices and learned to "see themselves as people with literate failure" (152). The situation described by Rogers is certainly much starker than anything the participants in my study face, but it illustrates the pervasive and powerful—violent, some would say—nature of dominant literacy (Stuckey 1991).

Accumulation is implicated in this discussion of how literacies are valued. As literacies accumulate, they vertically pile up in material forms and practices, old alongside new, and they horizontally spread out into life domains (Brandt 1995). One might expect this proliferation to be met with an expanded view of what it means to read and write. That is, the participants in this study and in the Pew Internet study could have considered more varieties of reading and writing valid, but they did not. Instead, we see an interesting conflict resulting from the accumulation of so many literacies. Brandt acknowledges the conflict inherent to accumulation, particularly as she makes this point, deserving further elaboration: "the history of literacy at any moment is always carrying along a complex, sometimes cacophonous mix of fading and ascending materials, practices, and ideologies" (666).

To expand on the notion that literacy carries a "complex, sometimes cacophonous" blend of ideologies, I want to continue Brandt's visualization of the horizontal development of literacy. As literacies spread out, they carry values with them and interact with the values of the life domains they are circulating within. As noted above, these values can be affected by dominant views of literacy, particularly the school-success narrative and the pedagogization of literacy. When new values and narratives become attached to these literacies, they influence the perceptions and practices associated with them. In all of this movement, literacies share space with and compete with other literacies; values clash, with some gaining privilege and support and others not. In the overall visual picture of accumulation, literacies rise and fall, spread out and circulate, and compete and sometimes collide. They get in the way of each other, and when some literacies hold more power—as a result of public policy, dominant narratives, cultural capital—in a particular domain, then they will most likely push away and marginalize other literacies with less power.

To make this visualization more concrete, I want to briefly present a narrative and counternarrative of Wikipedia, the online encyclopedia. One narrative attached to Wikipedia emphasizes its design as a democratic resource of knowledge, free and open for reading or contributing. This narrative celebrates the site's trust in the amateur, in the wisdom of the crowd, and in the transparent decisions and debates behind editing; it celebrates the site's ubiquity. A counternarrative attached to Wikipedia questions some of the same values: Should we rely upon the amateur? Should we trust the wisdom of the crowd? Is the site's ubiquity harmful, especially if it is unreliable? If a specific setting of literacy—such as a school—were to identify with and value the counternarrative, then Wikipedia would most likely be marginalized in that setting. Such narratives and responses to Wikipedia exist in far greater diversity than this brief sketch provides, but they hint at the "complex, sometimes cacophonous" discourses that accompany accumulated materials and practices (Brandt 1995, 666). Literacies have values, discourses, and narratives attached to them, which find differing degrees of acceptance and resistance in various domains of literacy.

A significant goal for composition has been to meet students where they are, to seek relevance with students' literacy practices outside of school. To that end, composition has expanded its definition of writing to include more forms and purposes in the classroom. As the expanded forms of writing come closer to reflecting the literate lives of students, it is hoped that students will have a more significant voice regarding how those literacies are understood and used in the classroom and beyond. That goal can be seen in Cynthia Selfe's (2009) statement describing how composition should value students' literacies:

> We need to better understand the importance that students attach to composing, exchanging, and interpreting new and different kinds of texts that help them make sense of their experiences and lives [. . .]. We need to learn from their motivated efforts to communicate with each other, for themselves and for others, often in resistance to the world we have created for them. We need to respect the rhetorical sovereignty of young people from different backgrounds, communities, colors, and cultures, to observe and understand the rhetorical choices they are making, and to offer them new ways of making meaning, new choices, new ways of accomplishing their goals. (642)

In this view, students and teachers can learn from each other to create new practices across a wide range of literate activities. Given the discussion in this chapter regarding students' perceptions of literacy and the conflict inherent in literacy accumulation, however, mismatches between the value teachers and students attribute to various literacy practices are bound to occur, sometimes in unexpected ways, as the following three examples demonstrate.

One mismatch occurs when teachers misunderstand students' digital literacy practices. Ellen Evans and Jeanne Po (2007) faced this problem when they assigned hypertext fiction with the "assumption that students steeped in the use of technology as a form of entertainment and play would be adept at the transition from print-based narratives to digital texts" (59). However, Evans and Po were surprised by how the hypertext fiction prompted "frustration and anxiety" from the students (57). The students were frustrated with hypertext fiction's unusual conventions and lack of closure. Complicating the view that the "millennial generation" values all forms of digital media, Evans and Po noted the students did not appreciate the combination of fiction and interactive clicking: "While they have grown accustomed to clicking on links and piecing together information from web searches, online databases, online newspapers, and so on, the students in this study wanted to reserve reading a book for *not* making decisions and not clicking on any links" (68, italics original). The students preferred reading fiction for the purpose of relaxation, not to take control of the narrative.[4]

An important observation from Evans and Po's (2007) study was that students bring a wealth of assumptions and expectations from their daily literacy practices into college. In this case, students' typical ways of reading print fiction and interacting with digital media created expectations that clashed with the expected ways of reading hypertext fiction in class. Conflicting expectations of literacy seem to be a byproduct of accumulation. When literacy practices—even those with which a student is familiar—cross a domain boundary, the values promoted by the teacher and those perceived by the student may come into conflict.[5]

In the Evans and Po account, teachers' and students' differing expectations for reading in a college course were in conflict. For Marvin Diogenes and Andrea Lunsford (2006), the conflict involved expectations for writing. Diogenes and Lunsford encountered this conflict as they revised the Stanford writing program to more fully incorporate oral, visual, and multimedia discourses. A new second-level course was added to the curriculum that asked students to perform research, develop arguments, and "reflect extensively on how to present or deliver their knowledge—what genre, media, and designs are called for in particular rhetorical situations" (146–7). The course demanded a lot from their students, and the teachers were unaware of how overwhelming it all was at the time. Diogenes and Lunsford observe that "in retrospect it's easy to see that we were to some extent dazzled by the possibilities presented to us, especially in the technology-enhanced classrooms specially designed for the [new] classes" (148). In the classes, students produced a variety of texts: videos, multimodal writing, audio essays, and web texts. In reviews and focus groups, the Stanford students remarked that they appreciated the chance to write in these new ways, but "they weren't sure their *writing* was actually improving. [. . .] So caught up were they in the fine points of Audacity or the pleasures of iMovies or the production of a zine that the actual writing (or at least what students understood as writing) in these endeavors seemed to suffer" (148, italics original). Here, what teachers and students "understood as writing" conflicted; the writing program drew from recently accumulated forms of writing to engage students in a wide range of practices when students (it seems) expected a more traditional form of writing. Although the program's intentions were good, it may not have prepared students for the conceptual change of what can count as writing in college.

In the final example, I want to suggest how the conflict between the values attributed to literate practices is not limited to what occurs in the classroom. As teachers, we sometimes underestimate the power we have as gatekeepers of literacy. We have the potential to reinforce and build upon the literacy strengths that students bring with them, drawing on these strengths for deeper engagement in and out of the classroom. Alternatively, we can overlook or even diminish these out-of-school literacies. For instance, I have been surprised by how, in a short period of time, students' views of Wikipedia changed so drastically. Within a few years, students switched from expressing admiration for the website to bashing its reliability. At least one significant reason for that switch has been their teachers' expressions of disdain for Wikipedia, particularly as a research resource in school. These pedagogical criticisms then get repeated by students, even in contexts outside of formal research projects. Indeed, when students and I discuss Wikipedia and other online knowledge resources in a class on information literacy, they explain how they have mocked (and have been mocked for) citing Wikipedia in online debates; the mockery commonly includes the argument that such a citation would not count in school, so it does not count in this out-of-school situation as well. Although I am glad that students have adopted a critical view of online information sources, I wonder whether the pendulum swing is an overcorrection.

Literacies accumulate, expanding the forms and practices of reading and writing. Yet, as this chapter has suggested, a relatively narrow view persists as to what counts as reading and writing. Previous educational experiences and cultural narratives shape students' views of what counts as reading and how to do various kinds of reading. As composition teachers incorporate more forms of reading and writing, particularly those that do not seem like typical school-based literacies, teachers may have difficulty aligning students' expectations with their own appreciation of what such literacies may offer.

NOTES

1   Certainly, writing teachers engaged out-of-school literacies well before the listed examples emerged. I am limiting my discussion to communication technologies because of their relation to accumulation and acceleration. However, I think such technologies did mark a significant shift in the attempt to "meet students where they are." Obviously, some

previous attempts involved assigning content familiar to students (life experiences, popular culture), but in the form of an essay—an unlikely genre for students' reading and writing outside of school.

2   Educational psychology research lends weight to the influence beliefs have on academic performance. After reviewing twenty years of research, Frank Pajares (2003) states that "an important pedagogical implication to emerge from these findings is that teachers would do well to take seriously their share of responsibility in nurturing the self-beliefs of their pupils, for it is clear that these self-beliefs can have beneficial or destructive influences" (153).

3   Jonathan Franzen's infamous slight against *The Corrections'* being chosen for Oprah's monthly book club is an interesting example of how the popular-literary divide played out in public.

4   In their explanation of students' resistance to hypertext fiction, Evans and Po (2007) also acknowledge the influence of reading for tests: "One result of our test-heavy education system is that students may not imagine any other way of approaching a text"; they then advise teachers to "consider the efficacy of a renewed focus on the act of reading and of making the kind of stance students take toward texts a focus of study and discussion" (70). Evans and Po recognize that many students probably bring a limited range of reading strategies to college and that teachers should intervene, not only with tools for reading, but also explicit discussion about how to construct reading in different ways.

5   Kip Strasma (2001) had an experience similar to Evans and Po's (2007) while teaching hypertext fiction. Strasma describes how the class struggled with hypertext fiction's different approach to narrative: "What I didn't realize at the time was how strongly hyperfictions directly juxtapose students' perceptions of order and duration, both of which are conditioned by print-based expectations. Because students and I expected hyperfictions to act like books, to conform to a common story-time within a singular discourse-time, we overlooked the opportunity to study directly both sets of unique characteristics" (270–271). Strasma's missed opportunity points to a way to make profitable use of conflicting literacies in the classroom. For Strasma, this experience suggests a larger question about digital texts in the classroom: "How do digital texts function in social, classroom settings? In what ways might they undermine or reconfigure expertise?" (258). Over a decade later, Stramsa's question about expertise is particularly relevant when educators tend to make general assumptions about students' digital expertise. Strasma's recognition of how expertise can be undermined and reconfigured in various ways deserves more investigation.

3

READING IN A CULTURE
OF ACCELERATION

"It is one of the great truisms of our time that we live in an
age of technological acceleration; the new paradigms keep roll-
ing in, and the intervals between them keep shortening."
– Steven Johnson (2010, 13).

Lauren read "tons of magazines": the print and online versions
of *Cosmopolitan, Time, Tennis,* and *Entertainment Weekly.* Every day
she sent dozens of text messages and checked in with her social
networking profiles. She consulted "various websites about
sports, about health tips and working out, learning better ways
to exercise and get physically ready [for games]." Although her
parents "are perfectly adequate with knowing how to work the
Internet," she still helped out sometimes: "I'm just faster and
less thrown off by pop-ups, and I've helped out with things, like
hotel[s] and flights and renting cars." When she and her family
traveled, Lauren would try to find an online version of "whatever English book I have to read at the time, [and] put it on
my laptop. That way, I'm not packing a bunch of books, and I
can put my own notes—in, like, bold words—right there on the
screen in the book. But then, I have to try and not play Solitaire
all the time."

Mark loved reading: "I read more than the average high
school student probably. I like fantasy and stuff like that, but
I also really like Hemingway and Shakespeare and classics, so
I try to hide my nerdiness with stuff of literary merit. My parents and relatives know that books are the best things to get for
me; they're what I like best." Mark tried to resist Myspace and
Facebook—"it all seems like an utter waste of time"—and the
web in general. However, he liked reading literature discussion

DOI: 10.7330/9780874219333.c003

forums, which he did not see as part of the web: "Not really. I mean, it's not empty gossip or people ripping on each other. It's a part of my [literary] reading. It has real value, subjects worth [the] time." Although he did not contribute to the discussion forums, he said the interpretations and conversations within deepened his appreciation and understanding of the novels. He seemed to view the online forum as an extension of his print reading, a significant part of how he made meaning.

Nadia read CNN, BBC, and several other online sites for national and international news. Her parents left Iraq when she was young: "Now I'm curious. What's it like there? How'd it get this way? I don't want to go there, and I don't remember it much, but that was my home." In the past few years she has read numerous historical books about the Middle East and contemporary accounts of the Iraq War. She supplemented the historical print books with online news: "It's interesting seeing the long [historical] perspective and the 'now,' the news from the Internet." In her reading on that subject, she moved between print and online texts. Without knowing she was in the study, two other participants named Nadia as the smartest, most confident student in their English class. Nadia enjoyed English class, read most of the assignments, but also turned to SparkNotes at times: "Sometimes there isn't enough time. I take shortcuts like everyone else."

These three participants live in a media-rich world. I selected only a few details from their interviews to highlight the range of literacy experiences, the back-and-forth shifts between print and online reading, and the connected use of diverse literacies to fulfill goals. In these three examples, we see how literacy has "piled up" in various forms and practices and "spread out" into various life domains (Brandt 1995). These features of participants' literacy practices support Deborah Brandt's claim that the "rapid proliferation and diversification of literacy" near the end of the twentieth century offers an "unprecedented" challenge for readers and writers who have to "piece together reading and writing experiences from more and more spheres, creating new and hybrid forms of literacy where once there might have been fewer and more circumscribed forms" (651). In

Brandt's estimation, being literate now "may be best measured as a person's capacity to amalgamate new reading and writing practices in response to rapid social change" (651). Brandt points to the importance of speed in this piling up and spreading out. Building on that foundational work, I argue that speed has become a defining feature of contemporary literacy. This is due to the rise of a culture of acceleration, a gathering of social, educational, economic, and technological forces that reinforce values of speed and efficiency. This chapter will explore how those values play out in how the students read at school, at home, and online.

SOCIO-CULTURAL INFLUENCES: NETWORK SOCIETY AND ACCELERATION

It may be tempting to point to various technologies as the reasons for changes in literacy, but technologies not only prompt but also combine with and respond to many cultural forces. We live in a culture that urges and thrives on speed and efficiency; capitalism demands getting rid of the old to make room for the new. New computers and cell phones seem obsolete when the latest version is released. Drive-thru options exist for food, medicine, money, and even alcohol. We pay bills and do banking online. Songs, television shows, books, and movies can be downloaded or streamed in minutes. As Internet users upgrade their connection speed, they wonder how they ever lived with the slower version. Digital cable allows viewers to record TV shows, fast forward through commercials, and watch two shows in about the same time it used to take to watch one. Mobile devices such as smartphones and iPads offer on-the-go, near-instant access to information, entertainment, and communication. The speeding up of everything (Gleick 1999) has reached such a degree that, like the Slow Food movement's reaction to fast food, people are forming "Unplugged" and "Off the Grid" movements that encourage people to decrease their use of electronic communication devices and to slow down the fast pace associated with constant connectivity.

Certainly, this is not the first time people have felt rushed by the speed of culture or overwhelmed by information. Karin Littau's (2006) *Theories of Reading* collects many of the "countless warnings" in the eighteenth and nineteenth centuries regarding the "epidemic" of "too much print, too much writing, too much reading" (4).[1] In *Fatal News*, Katherine Ellison (2006) explains how eighteenth-century authors created works that would "help citizens cope with the threat, real or imagined, of information overload" (110). Based on such examples, some could argue the current situation is not new. However, historical comparisons to our contemporary context are fraught with complexity and should be approached cautiously. For instance, in her historical examination of the reception of printing and the alarmed response to the overabundance of books, Elizabeth Eisenstein (2011) points out "it would be a mistake to take all such alarms [of information overload] too literally. Almost all of them were sounded by authors who were justifying the presentation of their own work to a presumably overburdened reader" (89). In many cases, these alarms were calling for the need to separate books of quality from bad books (27). It would be a mistake, I think, to reduce very different historical periods to a simple equivalence or to claim the current situation is nothing new. Growing historical evidence suggests the perception of "'information overload' is not a single and unitary phenomenon," but has been tied to different factors—quantitative, intellectual, cultural—at different times (Rosenberg 2003, 7–9). What has been understood as information and what has been deemed the cause of overload has varied. Historical comparisons, then, become even more difficult if the intention is to draw conclusions from very different situations. Ultimately, what matters for this project is a framework for understanding contemporary literacy, for negotiating the challenges and opportunities raised by accumulation and acceleration. In the historical work on information overload, the tendency now is to locate factors that have significantly affected the impression of overload and explore how those factors elicited responses from that time. Accordingly, as I make comparisons, they are merely to highlight significant contemporary factors, not to suggest a conclusion about the history of information overload.

Although Geoffrey Nunberg (1996) notes "[t]here has always been too much to read" (126), he argues the expansion of digital texts on the web has created a different situation for modern readers: the open publishing of the web makes the number of texts "genuinely unprecedented," and the open and easy access to information only increases "the impression of overload, rather than relieving it" (126). Nunberg's observation speaks to the paradox of literacy I described in the introduction: literacy enables and demands; technologies of literacy provide opportunities and conveniences but also expectations and challenges. Readers have access to more texts than ever before, but we are also aware of that many more texts. Readers navigate an increase in the number of texts, as well as the many shapes they take through different genres and media by the way those texts are packaged and distributed. This impression of overload can be daunting— as is the impression of acceleration, which is connected to the accumulation of texts and technologies of literacy.

The pervasive sense of acceleration is significantly different today because of the global network and a shared sense of speed. As Robert Hassan (2009) states, "Today, [. . .] we are *aware* of the shared experience of speed as never before. This is because the tempo of the pulsating dynamics of a globalizing world economy affects *more of us* at the *same time*, than ever before, and *more intimately* than ever before" (19, italics original). Although previous generations felt an accelerated pace of life, the difference is that their technologies did not "network tightly and rapidly like digital technologies do today" (38). Hassan builds his perspective of acceleration from Manuel Castells' (2010) concept of the "network society," which describes the transformation of social organization and social practice by transnational communication systems and the global economy. According to Castells, nearly every aspect of modern life has been influenced by this transformation of social networks into an interconnected, global system driven by the logic of the computer and the dominant practices of creating, processing, and transmitting information (21). An important development of the network society is our changing relationship to time, which has been caused, in part, by global capitalism and the culture of "virtual time," a shift away from clock time toward the combined sense of "timelessness" and "simultaneity" of online communication (491). The rise of the network society, Hassan (2009) argues, has led to a culture driven by speed: "The increasing *rapidity* at which we produce, consume and distribute commodities is now the core process, the central factor in the 'economy of speed.' This represents an immense *intensification* of the pace of commercial, technological, and organizational innovation—and a transformation of the cultural and social forms that spin out from its epicenter" (21, italics original).

These social and cultural ripples from capitalist and technological innovations can be difficult, if not impossible, to avoid. These innovations are not the simple cause of acceleration, which "*rises up* from the ways in which we interact and communicate across all walks of life" (Hassan 2009, 19, italics original); that is, the pace becomes woven into and develops further within existing practices. For instance, cell phones, e-mail, and social networking services (SNS) have made communication with friends and family easier over distance and time, but these same technologies also reinforce the value of constant availability, which then eases the transition for employee work hours to become more elastic and open-ended through the same communication channels. These practices become natural, part of daily life. As Hassan argues, developments like these lead to a "culture that increasingly makes no distinction between work and leisure, private and public, day and night, physical and virtual" (23). Speed and efficiency also lead to the expectation of flexibility with respect to the demands of the workplace and economic change, the construction of identity, one's physical location, etc.[2]

Speed is influenced by economic competition, which is also mirrored in social competition. Market competition for the latest communication technology or upgrade also drives the social competition to be an early user of the technology or upgrade, which then becomes the norm. People engage in "competitive consumption" (Heath and Potter 2004, 118) by purchasing the latest device to maintain or attain a particular social status and to gain a sense of technological advantage over others. Even if the sense of competition is not conscious, people might at least feel they could be more productive or successful—professionally, educationally, socially—if they kept up with the latest advancements. When consumption is not "competitive," it may be "defensive," such as when people buy larger, heavier vehicles as a protective measure against the increasing number of SUVs on the road (118). Similarly, people may feel compelled to acquire the newest, fastest technology when they see others possessing it (and whatever perceived edge accompanies it) or when their current device is not compatible with software updates or cannot handle increasingly heavy data processing. Increased consumption spurs more production and more updates, such as with the iPad, which was released in 2010, followed by the iPad 2 in 2011 and the iPad 3 in 2012. The sense of "keeping up" with technology, especially in terms of social capital, can be seen in the participant interviews discussed later in the chapter.

A significant means of faster production is the web as a platform for the development of genres and media. In *Where Good Ideas Come From*, Steven Johnson (2010) notes the decreasing intervals between when a technology is created and achieves widespread use: "It is one of the great truisms of our time that we live in an age of technological *acceleration*; the new paradigms keep rolling in, and the intervals between them keep shortening" (13, italics original). Johnson notes differences between how quickly a technology is built and achieves mass adoption in the twentieth and twenty-first centuries. Looking at technological change in the twentieth century, Johnson notes a regular rate of innovation and adoption, which he calls the "10/10 rule: a decade to build the new platform, and a decade for it to find a mass audience" (13). Using the twenty-first century example of YouTube, Johnson notes that it shattered the 10/10 rule, moving from "idea to mass adoption in less than

two years" (16). Not every successful web innovation moves at
the rate of YouTube, but many are much faster than the 10/10
rate. If we were to set the bar for mass adoption at 100 million users, MySpace reached it within three years (2003–2006),
Facebook in four years (2004–2008), and Twitter in five (2006–
2011). As the web expands, websites vie for attention and interaction; not only do new sites have to set themselves apart, but
existing sites continuously update and try to maintain a sense
of newness. With so many domains of life tied to online activity,
the speed of change on the web is a crucial part of the culture
of acceleration.

In a culture of acceleration, literacies appear, change, merge
with other literacies, and fade at a faster rate. As described
above, the first decade of the twenty-first century has witnessed
the arrival of forms of literacy that not only established themselves quickly but also became integrated into the daily lives of
many people. Forms of literacy and their practices rarely remain
static. In the case of Facebook, it has changed its format multiple times and merged other literacy practices—e-mail, instant
messaging, games—into its structure in an attempt to keep users
on the site. Such changes came from its designers, but change
occurs in other ways. For instance, the practice of text messaging does not have an owner or centralized location; when text
messaging practices change, they tend to occur through those
writing and reading the messages as they devise new expressions
and meanings to fit their purposes.[3] Forms of literacy fade, too,
even if they do not disappear completely. For instance, MySpace
and Second Life rose and fell quickly in popularity and use.
E-mail's function for personal communication has given way to
Facebook, Twitter, and text messaging. Blogging continues to
decline among teens, from 28 percent in 2006 to 14 percent in
2009 (Lenhart et al. 2010).

The acceleration of literacy doesn't just occur in how literacies appear, change, and fade, but also in how literacy practices
increasingly tend toward the value of speed. For instance, the
decline in long-form blogging may have been caused in part by
the rise of micro-blogging on Facebook and Twitter; readers and

writers probably perceive the shorter posts of micro-blogging as faster and easier, especially when mobile devices frame the context for reading and writing. Accumulation on the web stimulates acceleration; as the number of texts increase, as information expands, people respond with tools and methods of filtering information more quickly: search engines, personalized news feeds, crowdsourcing, skimming/scanning reading strategies, etc.

In the rest of this chapter, I examine how acceleration permeates the daily lives of the participants in two significant areas: the pace of school curricula, and the technologies that mediate participants' social interactions. I make important observations about how the participants read at school and at home, and about how and why popular social websites contribute to speed-based reading and writing. What appears is a complex picture. Accumulation and acceleration in school contribute to a curriculum driven by volume and speed, in which students feel pressured to get through material quickly and often shallowly. At home, most students use technologies that tend toward speed and brevity, yet they also read books and enjoy the slow, deep immersion offered by extended narratives. Online social interactions may be perceived as fleeting and shallow, yet the observations here reveal rhetorical choices that are sophisticated because of how they achieve continuous attention.

SPEEDS OF READING AT SCHOOL AND AT HOME

Diana juggles a part-time job, two sporting activities, and three advanced classes: "I work at Old Navy eight to fifteen hours a week, I run track, and I play field hockey for school (and I'm going to join a league that plays on Sundays), and I have two AP classes and college English, and I'm working on scholarships, so I'm busy with school a lot." Tim fenced three days a week and worked at a sports shoe store in addition to his course load. Amy worked twenty hours a week, played softball for school, and worked on scholarship materials while taking two advanced courses. The participants tended to overextend themselves,

taking on jobs, extracurricular activities, and volunteer positions. Many of them described their activities as beneficial for
getting into college and getting a good career. Compared to students who learn in struggling schools and live in economically
deprived areas, the participants in this study have what might be
called "good problems." With how important digital literacies
have become, scholars have urged critical attention toward the
digital divide, the unequal access to technology and the practices
associated with it, which can exacerbate existing educational and
economic inequalities (Banks 2006; Powell 2007). I think it's also
important to pay attention to the increased stakes of literacy for
students who are typically expected to do well. For many students,
college has become an expectation, an inevitable extension of
school on the path to a good job and a good life; increasingly, this
expectation means engaging in extracurricular activities, taking
Advanced Placement classes, and maintaining excellent grades.

The pace of reading in school is extra pressure for the
participants, with 15 to 20 books assigned per year. Midwest
High School has instituted a summer reading program, which
requires students to read four books over the summer, which
they then discuss in the opening days of the school year. As we
sat in the College and Career Center in the library, I asked each
participant "What challenges you as a reader in school, and
how do you respond to those challenges?" Every participant
responded in regard to the pace of the curriculum. Nadia commented on this pace:

> Freshman year was the first year we did summer reading. I didn't
> even know I could read that many books. We started right into
> it, with fifteen to twenty books a year. So, I read four books
> that summer. We went over two books in English class, and two
> books in other classes. Two weeks in, we were reading and writ-
> ing all the time. Every book we read, we'd finish in two weeks
> and then we'd write a paper. Then we'd read another book. You
> didn't have a break in between. We read *December Stillness*, wrote
> a paper; we read *Tuesdays with Morrie*, wrote a paper; read *As I
> Lay Dying*, we wrote a paper; read *Dr. Jekyll and Mr. Hyde*, wrote
> a paper; read *Frankenstein*, wrote a paper. Kept going and going
> and going.

Amy echoed Nadia's statements about the first year and added that the next year only increased the reading load: "Sophomore year in my English class, we were reading a book, reading a play, and writing something else all at the same time. So, I guess I learned to read three to four books at a time." Tim noted the pressure has continued through his senior year: "They urge things on us quickly. You have to have chapters one to six read by tomorrow, and we're going to have a quiz on it. I'm really busy all the time. I have fencing three days a week, work the other two days. As we talk about the readings in class, the teachers are all urgent: *Write this down. Circle that in your books.* And I can't do that. I can't read fast."

All of the students related examples like these; in other classes, students read textbook chapters with little instruction. The pace of instruction, the amount of time given to read, analyze, and write about texts, and the sheer volume of texts—these features of education did not reinforce focused reading, and they did not give students a sense of the variety of ways to read and how particular ways of reading can be used in certain situations. Reading was simply reading, and the students were asked to do a lot of it. There's also a significant contradiction in this educational model: read and learn quickly, but read and think deeply. None of the participants verbalized the contradiction in specific terms, but each expressed frustration regarding it.

David observed that one of his teachers liked to give the name "thinkers" to the readings that required careful analysis: "She'd say, 'This next reading is a thinker,' and I would just cringe. I didn't have time for that." Given David's self-image of a "bad reader," when he was given challenging material to read in a short time, he shut down and gave up. Rather than stop reading a book due to time constraints, several students said they would not even start. Tim noted it was a strange excuse, but one that made sense to him: "I'd rather side-step the whole issue of failing to read the assignment by not even starting it. That way, it's like a decision." James said he didn't like to read and discuss novels and poetry in the shallow ways demanded by the fast pace: "We would go through things so quickly, it could be a joke some days. So, some books I wouldn't even bother with. Wouldn't even open it. I mean, why take that seriously? I'm not going to spend a lot of time on something we're not going to go over much in class." However, unlike Tim, who did not seem concerned with hiding his lack of reading, James said there were ways to make it seem as if he had read: "You can pick up enough knowledge for a quiz late in the week if you were paying enough attention earlier."

Other students had devised tactics for reading a little bit of the text, just enough to get by. Sarah's frustration with the curriculum was a reason for taking shortcuts: "They expect you to love this stuff, to get really deep meaning out of it, but then we fly right through it. Why bother? The tests don't care as long as I get [the answer] right." Amy noted that when it comes to reading a book, "I have to finish what I start. So, if I run out of time, I'll just go check SparkNotes. I know some other students who read enough to get their one comment in during class, but I can't do that." I heard variations of Amy's tactic of reading supplemental commentary, which provided fodder for an in-class demonstration of knowledge that gave the appearance of having read. Mark stated, "You have a handful of people who read it, a select few who understand it—and they can talk about it. And then you have people who look at the SparkNotes and make stuff up based on that to try to convince the teacher they've read it." Laughing, he added, "I've done that before." A variation of this tactic was explained well by Diana, who did not have a problem keeping up with the pace; however, she had to adjust her usual ways of reading to do so: "I end up skimming a few chapters for what seems like an important part. The teacher will usually give enough context in the discussion for me to put together a comment that sounds smart." Nadia read most of the assignments, but also resorted to shortcuts: "I want to know what I'm talking about in class and what others are talking about. I don't want to look stupid. So, I read. I do a lot of it, and I somehow figure out how to get most of it done. But not all of it, and, yes, I use SparkNotes to fill in those gaps. Sometimes there isn't enough time. I take shortcuts like everyone else."

The fast-paced curriculum demanded a particular kind of reading: fast, shallow, and testable. In their own ways, the students recognized this kind of literacy was not worthwhile or that they could not read well under those conditions. In response, some simply decided not to read; others responded by devising particular reading tactics that seemed appropriate to the situation. Even at a good high school like Midwest High, the influence of state and federal testing increased the pace of the curriculum. Not only did teachers feel pressured to include more readings, but they also had to include more test preparation.

English teacher Julia commented on the dangers of raising the stakes on students so focused on achievement: "These kids are already involved in sports and scholarship activities to improve their college chances. Many of them work twenty hours [a week]. But state requirements keep being raised, and there's only so much they can do." Julia, with over twenty years of teaching experience, noted the pace of testing and teaching seemed to only get faster. Midwest High School consistently scored well in the state for reading and writing achievement. Julia was proud of this fact, but added ruefully, "They're very good at tests, and we've developed some sound pedagogy around that, but it's not always the best way to learn." From my observations of and discussions with Julia, I was amazed by what she managed to do despite the educational constraints under which she worked.

As much as the students liked their teachers and classes, most sounded disenchanted with the curricular focus on speed and quantity. Diana recalled when a teacher sheepishly recounted the events of *Macbeth* because the class had no time to read it, but it was on the class schedule and had to be covered: "The teacher seemed so embarrassed to do that, and we just played along and took notes." Many participants recalled the fast nature of class discussions over the readings, and noted how the class was trying to cover as many points as quickly as possible. These rapid-fire discussions could have contributed to Tim's feeling overwhelmed and disenchanted by urgent directions to "Write this down. Circle that in your books." They may also have contributed to David's dread of the "thinker" readings, especially if these difficult readings deserving of careful analysis could only result in quick overviews—and, later, quizzes and tests. When I asked students about reading in other classes, I heard similar stories about coverage and speed, with homework sheets and tests being the ultimate purpose guiding the reading. Describing non-English classes, Amy stated, "We go through it pretty fast. We're just supposed to read it, get done with it, and do the lesson." James had similar experiences: "We might talk about the content of the readings in history class, but it's just to check events and knowledge. There's no discussion of the reading itself. We have a lot of stuff to cover, so they [teachers] try to get us through it all." Sarah recalled several history classes in which the teacher would "rush us through chapters at times. We wouldn't even really pause to make sure it made sense. It felt like the plan, the schedule was tight with so much to do."

Despite their disenchantment with reading at school, nearly all of the participants—with the exception of David—expressed love and admiration for novels, placing their quality above magazines and Internet reading. It was surprising to hear how many students enjoyed reading leisurely—as long as they chose the books and how they read them. As they told these stories, the release from judgment, potential failure, and scheduled readings were underlying themes. Even though he was dodging reading assignments in class, Tim was no slouch at home, having read *The Iliad*, *Dante's Inferno*, and *Catcher in the Rye* in addition to the Chronicles of Narnia and the Lestat series by Anne Rice: "Sometimes I'll get on these reading kicks. I read Narnia in one weekend." James noted he could easily sit in his bed and read books for hours, "pulling all-nighters if I really get into it." The books were not short, either, with James listing Stephen King's The Dark Tower series and J.R.R. Tolkien's Lord of the Rings series as examples of books he would sink into for hours. Nadia stated reading at home motivated her to read her schoolwork faster: "Trying to enjoy and get the most out of school—yes, that's a good thing. There's so much more out there, though. At times I rush through homework so I can finish an assignment and move on to something I want to read on my own."

Nadia's preference for home reading over school reading was not unusual; and for most of the students, reading was not a solitary experience. Diana and Nadia described informal "reading groups" they had with friends: they would share books and often talk about them together at coffee shops. Although James was not a fan of web reading, he and Tim sometimes read web discussion forums for extra insights into King's and Tolkien's books. The participants told me many specific, affectionate stories about books they had read, including some non-fiction works. Nadia read history and travel books—travel was an important goal of hers—and she wanted to know more about the world: "There's so much out there, away from this. I can't really go yet. Reading about foreign places is a good way to prepare me and to keep that goal in mind." Diana was steeped in college-preparation books, wanting to "get a start on that [college]. I can't wait, and I intend on being ready to get the most out of that experience." Amy, Sarah, and Lauren read books, magazines, and websites about training for sports. Although David was not reading novels like the other eight participants, he had an extensive graphic novel collection that we talked about in detail, and, inspired by James Bond video games, he recently started reading books about the spy's author Ian Fleming.

On the one hand, these nine students can be seen as outliers: they went to an excellent high school, and they volunteered for a study about reading. On the other hand, they may not be that unusual: many students in my classes have openly admitted to shirking school reading while doing a healthy amount of self-selected reading. David Jolliffe and Allison Harl (2008) found similar reading habits in their survey of twenty-one first-year composition students at the University of Arkansas: "We found students who were actively involved in their own programs of reading aimed at values clarification, personal enrichment, and career preparation. In short, we discovered students who were extremely engaged with their reading, but not with the reading that their classes required" (600). The Midwest participants could be described in a similar way, with the exception that some participants were engaged with the class readings—only not at the pace and level of reading expected by the class. As noted earlier, several students finished reading some of the texts on their own terms, in their own time. The fact that Jolliffe and Harl's participants "defy the status-quo thinking that portrays first-year college students as incapable of and uninterested in reading" is worth emphasizing (607). The participants in my study were interested in reading, and they did a lot of it outside of school. Much like the participants in this study, Jolliffe and Harl's participants found school reading "uninspiring, dull, and painfully required" (611). For the Midwest participants, a significant element of the "painful" school reading was the pace and volume.

If the attitudes described above are more common than we may think, then what might that mean for how we assign reading? If students are actively reading at home even as they are actively dodging assigned reading, then how might the ways we teach reading contribute to such divided literacy practices? One school of thought is obvious: Students will always shirk school reading, will always find it "dull, and painfully required"; therefore, it's naïve to think a revised pedagogy could remedy an incurable fact of education. However, I would argue the purposes and strategies we teachers give—or do not give—to students have a major influence on not only how students read, but also whether students read an assignment at all. If that is the case, then perhaps we should pursue a different angle, not simply by finding more interesting readings or by imploring students to read, but by helping students *do more* with reading. What if students were given fewer readings and more support with strategies that could give them a wider range of experiences and understandings of those readings? What if the curricular trend toward accumulation—more objectives and assignments, more genres and media—creates shallow learning experiences for both reading and writing?

As Thomas Newkirk (2009) states, a problem with modern education is curricular "clutter—the piling on of objectives and requirements—that makes any form of sustained work difficult" (11). The clutter pours in from many sources and can be found at any level of education: calls for accountability and testing, which have been "ratcheting up the frequency and stakes of testing systems" since the 1990s (Supovitz 2009, 215–16); the perceived need to train students for both the workforce and future coursework; the remediation of skills; the increase in disciplinary knowledge and skills, which further expands the discipline's sense of what is important and necessary to cover; the increase in textbook length, which covers more topics and improves its chances of being adopted while pressuring teachers to use more of it; and the expansion of genres and media that complicate what it means to be a literate person in the twenty-first century.[4] Anyone putting together a first-year composition syllabus or working with a committee to revise the composition curriculum has recognized how multiple objectives and goals clamor for attention. Of course, *clutter* is a pejorative term to use for such considerations when many of them seem so important. Yet, without the ideal vertical curriculum—a hard-won reality— trying to pile on so many objectives into one or two semesters does make a composition course feel, well, cluttered. These sources of clutter are only some of the ways in which literacy accumulates in materials and practices as students and educators respond to the ever-changing literacy demands of various social institutions.

As curricula take on more texts and more objectives, teachers and students proceed through them at greater speeds. This is acceleration, an imperative of "network society" (Castells 2010; Hassan 2009). Earlier in this chapter, I referred to Hassan's description of a rapidly spinning "epicenter" of "commercial, technological, and organizational innovation" that transforms social life (21); education has not been immune to this transformation. Looking over twentieth-century literacy education, Deborah Brandt (2004) sees a kind of acceleration in education as literacy became "a means of production in a capitalist economy," subject to the "logics of competition," which place no "limit on better, faster, cheaper, smarter means to an end"

(496–97). The demands of literacy keep rising to fit changing economic and technological needs, and everyone must keep up or fall behind. Students and educators chase after the latest technological development, the latest set of skills needed to thrive in workplaces that require flexibility (Hassan 2009) and adaptability to changing literacy practices. In Brandt's (2004) estimation, the various pressures put on schools are "especially crushing," and they haven't been helped by governmental interventions, such as No Child Left Behind, which are guided by rules of production and competition that aim "to speed up the race, not equalize the pace" (500).[5] In the wake of No Child Left Behind, the competitive race of education continues in reform attempts. With metaphors of competition and speed built into the title, Race to the Top encourages the expansion of charter schools as a "competitive mechanism for innovation in public education," and it contains "provisions for high stakes testing [that] are more stringent than those in NCLB" (Shannon and Goodman 2011, 6). The shape of secondary education should matter to college teachers not only because of how students' educational experiences influence their practices in college, but also because of the increasing calls to more tightly integrate high school and college. Although multiple voices are calling for smoother transitions between high school and college, Kristine Hansen and Christine Farris (2010), note "educational institutions and state governments [are] pay[ing] growing heed to the businesses and private foundations urging the integration of high school and college" (xx). In their examination of this trend, Hansen and Farris observe that first-year composition has been marked as "appropriate to move into the high school to speed up student development and make room in college for other kinds of learning" (xxii). With the goal of getting students into the workforce more quickly, high school-college integration involves the need to propel students through school faster, which can be seen in Advanced Placement courses, accelerated programs, and early college high schools.[6]

School was not the only place where students experienced the effects of acceleration. The participants also felt rushed and overwhelmed by some of their personal online reading and writing practices. As much as they enjoyed their social technologies, they also felt pressured and even annoyed by them. The interview excerpts that follow reveal the rhetorical choices the participants made in response to the pressure they felt to keep up.

THE SPEED OF KEEPING UP

The participants recognized the value of speed and efficiency in their online activities. When I asked them about what they usually read online, nearly all of them described a routine: certain sites in a certain order. Few wandered aimlessly around the web. Amy said, "I just go to certain sites to find what I need or want, but I don't just go and read anything. I feel like it's below my reading level, not much complexity." James regarded the web as something "to search quickly and leave. It hurts my eyes. I'd rather read a book." Sarah noted "I have sites favorited [sic] that I go through, usually in order—bam—and then I'm done." Most students saw the web as a tool to get things done quickly.

As I interviewed the participants, I tried to stay mindful of the fact they were in the high school library's college preparation room with me, a college teacher, and that they volunteered for a study about reading. I worried that they were telling me what they thought I wanted to hear. Even after I assured participants that I enjoyed pop culture and spent a lot of time on the web, they maintained their previous statements about limited online engagement. However, when I asked about some of their favorite sites and how long they would spend on them, the stories about speed and efficiency changed slightly. Lauren talked about "losing time" while browsing magazine and sports websites: "I don't mean to spend so much time online, but after a while, you look at the clock and wonder how an hour went by." Nadia described the detailed reading she does of international news websites: "I read CNN and BBC news sites. That can take some time—a lot of news in the world, you know. I can lose track of time doing that." Mark revealed how much he enjoyed reading others' viewpoints on literature discussion forums: "Reading what others have to say can be really enlightening. And they [the forum participants] can be anybody, not only students. There's a lot of adults and older people on those websites, and it's cool to hear these different viewpoints. I don't always agree with them, but I like seeing things in new ways."

In addition to describing various levels of online engagement, the students also expressed mixed feelings about technology. Participants repeatedly talked about social technologies in terms of appreciation and frustration. They loved what technology offered: the multiple options for keeping in touch with friends and family, the potential to share information in different ways, and the opportunities to create online identities. However, they also expressed frustration regarding these things they took delight in. Participants kept talking about the need to "keep up"—with the latest technology, with the text messages sent by friends, with online social network events that affected their offline lives. Tim felt left out after he failed to keep up with online life when "typical high school drama" occurred on various students' profile pages, which he didn't get to see: "Our Internet at home wasn't working for a few days, and I went to school and didn't know what anyone was talking about. All these conversations were happening, they were based on stuff that happened online, and I was just trying to catch up. It was crazy. It was like I missed a really important [TV] episode."

Whereas Tim missed a social experience, Diana expressed frustration with being too connected. This frustration came out of a discussion we had regarding communication choices. First, she compared text messages and e-mail to instant messages: "I wouldn't do something really important over e-mail, like something that was seriously emotional because it's so easy to be mistaken. Messengers, though, let you use a lot of smileys, and when you use different fonts, you know they're going to transfer the right way." When I asked more about this preference, she expanded on how misunderstandings could happen so easily with text messaging: "It's hard to know if others are being sarcastic or mad or funny. Tone is hard to get, vowels are missing. And it's not like LOL [laughing out loud] really means LOL all the time. It's great that it's fast, easy, but that can also be frustrating." The unclear communication and speed of text messaging increased the chances that "it can all go wrong so fast. And you don't want to leave people waiting, so you reply fast without a lot of thought. That's not always the best way to reply. Feelings get hurt. Misunderstandings happen. Then you end up spending more time fixing all that." Diana sounded amused and annoyed as she described these frustrations, laughing and sighing throughout. The mobility of text messaging posed another problem for Diana. As she stated, "At least with instant messengers, you could be 'Away.' You could type an 'Away' message and others were okay with that. You can't be 'Away' from your cell phone." Diana then described her cell phone as a "chain" that kept her bound in some ways: "I mean, I love it. But it does tie you down. That's annoying when you want to be alone—you know, offline, in a way. But then you don't want to miss out on things or have your friends bothering you about not getting back to them."

Other participants echoed Diana's complaints, and I saw David's dismissive, annoyed response to the expectation of constant availability. During my interview at David's house, he briefly checked text messages that kept buzzing in, but did not immediately respond: "It's just stuff from friends. They might get mad that I'm taking so long to respond, but they'll get over it." Although David casually dismissed his friends' potential anger, he admitted they've gotten angry before: "I'm not exaggerating about that. If I don't respond quickly, they think I'm, like, trying to ignore them. It all goes away, but it's still stupid drama for a few minutes. Thankfully, my parents aren't that bad about it. I have some friends—their parents are always calling, and they [the parents] get seriously worried when they [David's friends] don't answer." Many students in my classes—from freshman composition to upper-level courses on media studies and writing technologies—have written about and discussed in class this same love-hate relationship with information and communication technologies. They want to stay in contact with their friends and family, they want to stay informed on the latest news (whether gossip or serious), and they appreciate the ability to do so, but they also feel the pressure to do so.

The need to stay connected and keep up with technology resulted in participants' buying new devices and adapting to new practices. Lauren complained she could not keep up with her friends' text messages and blamed "the buttons on the phone. They're fine if you make a call [with them], but they fail at texting. The buttons get stuck, or they don't flip through the letters well—and then I have new texts waiting for me and I'm still trying to write that [first] one. My friends get mad, and I feel stupid. So, I've been begging my parents, and they're finally getting me [a new] one with the little keyboard." Although Sarah appreciated the speed of technology, she also felt left out by not keeping up with various changes: "My friends keep getting new phones, and then I want a new one. Or they'll be talking about these funny or awesome websites—I've never heard of them. I don't have time to play around like that. It's all great when I have time, but I'm busy. It's a pain sometimes." Other participants talked in similar tones about needing to buy new computers or learning how to navigate the web on a cell phone; they were happy, in some regard, with the newness of it all, but also frustrated at the need to keep up with the latest development.

As the next section illustrates, the drive to "keep up" also influenced participants' reading and writing choices with these social technologies. Acceleration reinforces literate behaviors and rhetorical choices that value speed and efficiency. Although the stakes of the writing may seem low, and the particular writing choices may strike some as unsophisticated, I think such choices are interesting largely because they are ephemeral: they are not the types of reading and writing we teach, and they involve quickly formulated rhetorical decisions that can be read by dozens, even hundreds of people.

ACCELERATION IS A RHETORICAL FORCE

The influence of acceleration could be seen in students' need to continuously update their personal profiles on social networking sites. Diana said, "I feel like I should update my page often. Friends come to check it out, and if it's the same old thing all the time, that's disappointing. So, I try to post updates or pictures, even if they're not that great." In college, David said he wanted to keep friends coming back to his Facebook page, so he would "put up crazy pictures and say stupid things on purpose. I'm not asking for attention. You just have to keep it fun." Tim felt like he should write comments on people's Facebook walls more often so they would comment on his in return: "I didn't have much activity on my Facebook for a while, so I figured I'd write things on others' walls, and they'd do the same to mine. It worked. And they [Tim's comments] weren't anything special, just basic stuff—'how's it going?' and things like that." Other students described a similar need to "keep up" with their profile pages and to keep them interesting for readers.

As Bronwyn Williams (2009) observes, when students talk about tweaking and updating their blogs and personal profiles, their concerns about "keeping an audience interested and entertained" mirror those that "preoccupy mass media producers" who have to continuously create fresh, new products (85). Williams' observation is striking when recalling Tim's comment about how missing a few days of Internet socializing was akin to missing an important TV episode. This desire to constantly update is also mirrored by the attention-keeping practices of Facebook itself, which has a monetary interest in keeping users logged in as long as possible. This is why Facebook has incorporated games, chat, and e-mail; reminds users to contact friends and make more friends; and pushes the update system to notify friends when a picture has been added or any kind of status element has been changed. Students have internalized these attention-getting, attention-keeping practices, which are not only imbued with value by Facebook and MySpace, but also by a range of media experiences that have allowed "regular folk" to receive mass attention: Twitter, reality TV, YouTube, web comments that get quoted on TV news, etc. In a culture of acceleration and information overload, attention has immense value because so many competing options exist for gaining that attention. As

Colin Lankshear and Michele Knobel (2003) argue, the ability to "attract, sustain, and build attention" is important in this "attention economy" (109) and will be a "potent catalyst" for the development of new literacy practices (110).

The participants performed and practiced a daily, ephemeral rhetoric with their attempts at attracting and sustaining attention on their social websites. The initial attraction of attention seemed to be what mattered most to them: How can I get people to read this? The sustained attention was not for the comment or the update or the picture itself, but for the profile page; the rhetorical act seemed to be a means to an end, one of many ongoing attempts at attracting and re-attracting attention. And, even for the profile page, sustained attention was not the ultimate goal. Instead, the rhetorical acts needed to be persistent to stimulate reoccurring attention. The participants acknowledged they must "keep up" with updating the profile: "Yeah, I try to post stuff often because then your page just seems busier and more interesting to visit, to check out a lot instead of just once a month," said Diana. The participants said they didn't expect visitors to stay long, just long enough to "see the new thing," in Tim's representative words. These were rhetorical acts designed around speed and fleeting attention.

Acceleration is a rhetorical force, shaping multiple authorial choices, with delivery being especially influenced. Delivery, one of rhetoric's five canons, has been largely ignored due to its attachment to speech, which has faded as a pedagogical concern for composition instructors (Porter 2009, 207). In his resuscitation and theorization of delivery for digital contexts, James Porter describes the component of distribution/circulation, which involves "the technological publishing options for reproducing, distributing, and circulating digital information" (208). The first part of that component, distribution, is "the initial decision about how you package a message in order to send it to its intended audience"; the second part, circulation, is the potential for the message to "be re-distributed without your direct intervention" (214).[7] What I find interesting about the students' rhetorical choices is how acceleration (which

Facebook both reflects and feeds into) influenced a concern for fresh and recurring distribution and not a concern for circulation. Certainly, one could assume the participants would have been happy if a post had circulated, especially if it were something clever that traveled orally through school. Indeed, the students enjoyed the positive feedback they received online, but they claimed many of their updating choices were made for the sake of updating, for the sake of keeping up. As David said, "Some people you can tell put a lot of thought into what they do on Facebook, but they look like they're trying too hard." Diana conveyed a similar sentiment, and then assessed how many of "my contributions aren't winners. I just want people to know I'm still alive and around. That's all I have time for a lot of the time." Although I think the students put more thought into these acts than they claimed (a point I'll return to), they were largely focused on "What now?" instead of "How effective and lasting can this be?" This was a rhetoric aimed at fading.

The participants downplayed how much thought they put into their choices of updates, pictures, and wall posts. With my experience teaching courses on technologies of popular culture, I'm used to hearing students minimize how important or involved their interactions are with Facebook and blogs. Even among other students, the refrain "It's just the Internet" is a popular phrase that makes one appear appropriately distanced. Such distancing and minimizing of effort is not unusual. Certainly, when a participant would post a simple "Hey, how's it going?" on someone's wall, that probably did consist of minimal effort. However, many of the participants' rhetorical choices were actually fairly sophisticated, even though they weren't aware of it.

As the participants described their choices, they would emphasize their "silly" or "not too serious" nature. David often used quotes from *The Simpsons, South Park,* and *Family Guy* as updates or wall posts. He showed me one recent post he made to a friend's wall: "My cat's breath smells like cat food." He mentioned a few others—"if we're still alive in the morning, then we're not dead" (*South Park*); "this is not how a human being is supposed to look" (*Family Guy*)—and said this in response to my question about why he used them: "They're just easy and fast. People know them. If they don't, they at least know that you're making a random reference. That's funny by itself. People like those things, and it's easier than coming up with something of your own on the spot, you know, at the time. So, when I want to do something fast and stupid, I do that." Although the decision seemed obvious to David, a lot of thought went into it: What does my Facebook audience like? What can I do quickly, without much original effort? What makes me seem funny and casual? He knew pop culture references fit the necessary tone and audience expectations, and the light tone didn't just extend to wall posts and updates. As David said, "I wouldn't start a 'Save the Whales' group [on Facebook] or anything like that. Maybe 'Save the Mullet.'"

This light tone was recognized by others. Nadia said, "I would never start a political debate on someone's wall." She knew the tone had to be casual, which would lead to "frivolous and funny and meaningless stuff that I do with pictures and things I write on there." Tim observed that serious pictures—of family or hobbies—probably wouldn't "fly well" on Facebook: "If I do put them up, I'd have to put some bland or nonsense pictures to lessen their effect." Sarah and Amy said they and their friends often used (in Amy's words) "song lyrics we like" as "a kind of shorthand reference" in their wall posts and updates. Diana said a lot of her decisions about making updates and wall posts were based on the perceived light tone of Facebook: "Facebook seems built for light interaction. No one wants Internet drama. They don't want to hear that you're genuinely having a bad day. So, you have to put a light spin on it." She showed me her latest update: "Confused by lunch. Seriously. Lunch." I asked her about the update, and she said, "I was actually having a rough day. Lots of stuff was going on, and I started to make two different things for lunch—made one, didn't eat it, started making another. So stupid and really frustrating, but I made it something funny even though it wasn't really that funny for me." From reading so many examples of successful posts, Diana recognized the constraints of the genre and wrote her update accordingly.

Although the participants downplayed their involvement and their writing, they were making complex rhetorical decisions that only seemed simple because they had internalized the discourse rules for the website. They exhibited awareness of *kairos*, which involves choosing the best discourse for the situation, taking into consideration timing, audience, and context. How did they become aware of these discourse rules? I asked participants if they ever made rhetorical missteps in their Facebook interactions. They mostly avoided, in Amy's representative words, "saying something regrettably stupid" by reading what others did and noting what worked and what did not. They lurked, reading wall posts and updates and looking at pictures, figuring out how it worked: "With something so public, I know my friends and I just kept looking at it before actually doing anything," Amy said. She then explained some of the pitfalls of "regrettable" pictures or posts, adding, "It all moves so fast, and you can do something stupid just as fast." Lauren and her friends figured out the discourse rules together: "I totally forgot about that [until now], that we hung out for a while [on Facebook] not doing anything but seeing what others did and saying 'Oh, that's how you do that, and don't do that.'" Sarah and David were exceptions; they participated without delay, a move partially inspired by the quick nature of the medium: "My friends and I just tried stuff out, and if it was wrong or dumb—no big deal. It'd be gone soon," Sarah said. David also commented on this: "More mistakes are on the way. Others say stupid things, post a private picture to everyone. What I did will be forgotten yesterday." When reading the "stupid" posts by others, the participants reflected back on what they had written and realized the fast pace of online writing could be forgetful and forgiving.

For the most part, the participants read examples to learn and internalize discourse rules, and from this reading they sensed the influential force of acceleration on distribution and *kairos*: make the message brief, light in tone, and tied to pop culture if possible so its effects are immediate and innocuous; and maintain fleeting but reoccurring attention. In the participants' activities, reading and writing were cooperatively linked, mutually reinforcing. They read models of what and how to write, and they wrote and thought about how it might be read by others. The practice of imitating models and the cooperative relationship between reading and writing will return in chapter five.

FAST AND SLOW RHETORICS

This ephemeral rhetoric is interesting when put in the context of the remix, which seems designed for circulation. Remix is not only a popular feature of online communication, but also a popular subject of scholarship and pedagogy (Dubisar and Palmeri 2010; Jenkins 2008; Lessig 2008). A remix recombines elements of an existing text, or mixes the elements of two or more texts. For instance, the remix video "Synchronized Presidential Debating" illuminates the rehearsed talking points by Barack Obama and John McCain during the three 2008 presidential debates, cutting and blending the talking points across the debates to illustrate how these events rarely offer any fresh insights regarding the candidates. If the remix uses combination and juxtaposition in surprising and effective ways, it is more likely to spread, to circulate. As remixes circulate, they inspire more remixes—either with the same texts or with similar texts. After musician will.i.am remixed the words from Barack Obama's concession speech in the New Hampshire presidential primary into the music video "Yes We Can," the concept and structure was remixed into two satirical videos of a pessimistic John McCain, one titled "No, You Can't." Such political remix videos started to gain notoriety a few years earlier with a remix of President George W. Bush's third State of the Union Address, which edited his words into fluid statements like "Our first goal is to show utter contempt for the environment." Other videos remixed the address in various ways, and the authors of the videos often included a link to a previous remix that inspired them.

Although the popularity of remixes testifies to the driving force of circulation, an increasing amount of digital delivery seems to be concerned with immediate and ephemeral distribution. Twitter and text messages are the most obvious examples. Just as the students might have enjoyed a Facebook post being circulated, many Twitter users hope to have their words retweeted, which might gain more attention and new followers. This obvious goal of Twitter should not be overlooked. However, it seems to me that many daily tweets are created with the same ephemeral design as the participants' Facebook posts: something inconsequential to maintain recurring attention. This other goal of Twitter also should not be overlooked. Acceleration encourages continuous movement, not always for the objective of remaking, but often for pushing aside the old and making room for the new. Along with remixes and other exemplars of rhetorical circulation, ephemeral distribution seems to be a prominent form of contemporary digital delivery.

What might be the value of studying such rhetoric? Lester Faigley (2006) begins to answer that question by articulating two oppositions, the struggle between "fast rhetoric"—e-mail, instant messaging, digital images, websites—and "slow rhetoric," which is what we typically study and teach (4). Indeed, Faigley argues against fast rhetoric, associating it with "a culture that suffers from attention deficit disorder, a culture where things are quickly used and discarded" (9).[8] He compares its characteristics with those deemed more valuable in slow rhetoric: "In fast rhetoric, rapid fire, visual intensity, wit, and originality win out over lengthy exposition, explicit logical relations, sobriety, and order" (4). After discussing the increasing pace of information glut and communication technologies, Faigley urges the teaching of slow rhetoric: "We need to make better arguments about the value of slow rhetoric and be more imaginative about creating spaces where slow rhetoric can be practiced. The fate of future generations will depend on how well the students we teach can use slow rhetoric" (9). I agree with Faigley that scholars and teachers should work harder to make the case—to students, to the public—that logical, respectful, and informed discourse is worth learning and practicing. Beyond that point of agreement, though, I wonder what opportunities the field might miss if it does not pursue the benefits of fast rhetoric. How might we view fast and slow rhetorics more productively?

The binary division of fast versus slow rhetoric could instead be viewed as a continuum: communication choices vary along a range of slower rhetorics and faster rhetorics. For certain purposes and audiences, slower rhetorics work well; for others, faster rhetorics would be more appropriate. One problem with adopting faster rhetorics into our pedagogies is that we are so familiar with slow rhetoric: "We know how to teach slow rhetoric and what slow rhetoric can accomplish" (Faigley 2006, 7). That is, we are comfortable teaching reading and writing of alphabetic, print-based texts, and we are familiar with extolling the virtues of academic arguments. We are less familiar with faster rhetorics, we are not as comfortable teaching them, and we are probably less certain about what they can accomplish. If we do not know what faster rhetorics can accomplish, then how can we dismiss them?

In an age of accumulation and acceleration, when it is almost required to communicate across a range of technologies, a responsible pedagogy may involve teaching a range of rhetorical speeds. Students, employees, and citizens often need to turn a slower rhetoric into a faster rhetoric, such as condense a large amount of research into a short paper and then a presentation, or encapsulate a complex protest movement with tweets and hashtags, physical signs and symbols, oral chants and songs. Sometimes wit can cut through a bad argument better than sound logic. The powerful image, the personal example, the emotional plea—we can all think of instances when these have been more effective than a carefully presented set of claims and evidence.

Nancy Welch (2011) offers an interesting perspective on slow/fast rhetoric in her examination of working-class labor rhetoric. Welch's primary argument is that the middle-class rhetoric we teach in class—the academic argument, the print essay—is too limited for the working-class realities we and many students face. Although she does not characterize her work in these terms, her examples and claims speak of the need for both slow and fast rhetorics. When Welch and her colleagues organized to protest university budget cuts, they first employed "academic argumentative moves" that were stifled. Then, they turned to a louder, faster rhetoric to gain attention: "But finding those [academic] arguments cordoned off into the academy's version of free speech zones—three minutes of public comment time at a board of trustees meeting—we have also needed to learn to march into trustees meetings with chants and bullhorns, and to understand such tactics not as impropriety but as the exercise of our means, our authority to make space so that what we say can be heard" (237). Welch points to the historical example of the Industrial Workers of the World (IWW), who used "print literacy *plus* political cartoons, radical iconography, and their 'little red song book' to knit together a multiracial, multilingual working class from New England textile mills to West Coast logging camps" (237, italics original). In her public writing class, Welch asks students to experiment with multiple rhetorical forms, including slogans and chants (238). Welch's pedagogy is an exemplary model of how to introduce a range of rhetorical speeds and demonstrate that fast rhetorics and slow rhetorics fulfill different purposes.

NOTES

1   Karin Littau (2006) also ties these warnings to early twentieth-century concerns about the dangers of film; one being that the new visual form would undermine the pleasure taken from books.

2   For more on capitalism and speed, see Ben Agger (2004), who coined the term *fast capitalism.*

3   The changing technologies that support text messaging undoubtedly have an influence on the practice. Cell phone keyboards and voice-to-text applications are only two technological developments that have altered the speed and convenience of text messaging. However, such changes are not the same as when Twitter makes a central, formative change to its site.

4   College is not immune to curricular clutter. Colleagues in history and science have told me about the increasing size of textbooks and how they feel the need to cover more content. Composition has felt the pressure, too, with new practices of multimodal composition competing with existing print-based expectations of first-year composition.

5   See David Tyack and Larry Cuban (1995), and Angela Green (2009) for more on how education became linked to business interests, efficiency models, and the economic health of the country.

6   Hansen and Farris (2010) note "such an integrated educational system would require that K–12 and postsecondary systems (1) assume joint responsibility for defining standards, curricula, expectations, and assessments; (2) share seamless accountability, finance, and governance systems; and (3) create multiple pathways to a postsecondary credential" (xx).

7   Jim Ridolfo and Dànielle Nicole DeVoss (2009) articulate a variation of circulation in their concept of "rhetorical velocity," which involves thinking ahead about how one's text might travel, get picked up by others, and be recomposed by them in ways that may or may not reflect the original intentions or goals.

8   Although Faigley (2006) does not draw from Castells or Hassan, he links his discussion to acceleration, noting that what makes current instances of fast rhetoric different from previous versions "lies in how [they] are embodied in larger cultural trends. The proliferation of digital technologies since 1990 has accelerated the pace of global capitalism, uncertainty, complexity, and individualism" (4).

4
DIRECTING ATTENTION
Multitasking, Foraging, Oscillating

"We're drowning in [information]. What we lack is the
human attention needed to make sense of it all."
– Richard Lanham (2006, xi)

David has a multimedia coffee table. On the couch, he's within
reach of a cell phone, iPod, Superman comic, *Car and Driver*
magazine, the newspaper, John Grisham's *Bleachers*, an Xbox
wireless controller, and the remote to a big-screen TV. I can
barely see the glass top of the table underneath the layers of
media. As we talk about his reading practices, ESPN mutely
flashes text and statistics and talking heads on TV, his cell phone
vibrates on the glass countertop three times with text messages
from friends, and he plays the Internet game *Fish Eat Fish* on his
laptop, which also has web browsers open for Addicting Games,
eBay, and ESPN. David tells me *Fish Eat Fish* can be played in a
few minutes and does not require any significant investment, so
he can abandon it at any time to restore eBay's screen for the
latest bid, or ESPN's screen for more information on anything
the television broadcast failed to provide. He had turned off
the Instant Messenger (IM) screens upon my arrival, saying they
would have been too distracting during our interview.

Looking at his room, I noticed David has nearly every con-
ceivable medium at his fingertips. I also noted that these media
competed for his attention. In the midst of this media-saturated
room, David alternates his attention from one medium and
genre to another, but how does he make sense of information
when it arrives in such a tidal flow?

DOI: 10.7330/9780874219333.c004

Because of situations like the one I just described, scholars have become interested in "attention economics," arguing that when information abounds, what is most valuable is attention. In 1971, economist Herbert Simon claimed "a wealth of information creates a poverty of attention and a need to allocate attention efficiently among the overabundance of information sources that might consume it" (Simon 1971, 40–1). Of course, Simon made this statement two decades before 24-hour TV news and the World Wide Web, and three decades before 500-channel digital cable, ubiquitous cell phones, and millions of blogs and billions of web pages. More recently, Richard Lanham (2006) argued that all of this information requires better filters, with rhetoric being one of the most effective filters. Lanham claims rhetoricians have a special place in this attention economy because rhetoric is primarily concerned with gaining and directing attention (xii–xiii). In a similar vein, Colin Lankshear and Michele Knobel (2003) explain how new literacy practices can be used to gain attention. In these turns toward attention, however, the issue of how readers direct and spend their attention has been overlooked.

This issue is central to composition classrooms, which tend to value slow, sustained reading. Whether a student is reading a short story or an essay, each text is an unfolding of meaning constructed as the reader carefully attends to every paragraph and page. Classroom discussions typically depend upon this kind of reading; otherwise, silence fills the room after a few students offer a response to the "gist" of the reading. Effective student essays also grow out of that focused reading, with literary and rhetorical analyses depending upon precise attention to detail: shades of meaning, contextual consideration, and connections of parts to whole.

Yet, what are we as teachers leaving out if we see this kind of reading as the only valid one—or simply as the best kind of reading? It seems irresponsible not to think more broadly about many forms of reading and how students could benefit from them. In 1999, after recognizing differences between online and print reading, James Sosnoski (1999) wrote that compositionists should pursue a pedagogical praxis for "hyper-reading," but worried teachers would resist these new forms of reading because of a perceived lack of "coherence, substance, and depth" (173). Given how little attention digital reading has received in composition, it seems Sosnoski's fears were justified. In Scott DeWitt's (2001) work on teaching hypertext reading and writing, he observed that his students' web reading tended to be fleeting, resulting in momentary reflections on texts and hardly any connections between texts (140–45). DeWitt offers a "reflective model" of hypertext reading, which asks students to write reflections on the websites they visit, slowly creating summaries and connections. Although the reflective model is one good approach, this book's argument is that readers need to be more versatile, able to use a repertoire of reading strategies that vary in speed and depth. Slow, fast, shallow, and deep readings—and all of the degrees in between—are shaped by choices of attention.

This chapter focuses on three case studies of attention. During interviews and observations in their homes, David, Tim, and Diana engaged in online reading. David's case study brought up the issue of multitasking. In his room, he switches among various tasks and texts, devoting different degrees of attention to each as he does so. From my observations of David, I develop a heuristic for teaching and studying multitasked reading. I also complicate popular notions that multitasking is bad for learning. With Diana and Tim, I am more interested in how they read across websites, using forms of reading I describe as foraging and oscillating. As the chapter develops, I also complicate the binaries of attention/distraction and hyper/deep attention, moving toward a more nuanced view of each.

MULTITASKING

A significant aspect of modern reading is multitasking, which allows people to manage more than one task simultaneously or through alternate task switching (Lin, Robertson, and Lee 2009). Multitasking isn't a new activity, but what makes it significant today is the degree to which it happens and the complex technologies that enable and promote it. David's room is a fine example of this, and it may not be that unusual. According to a 2009 Kaiser Family Foundation Study (Rideout, Foehr, and Roberts 2010), eight- to eighteen-year-olds use media 7.5 hours in a day, using multiple media simultaneously to allow them to "pack a total of 10 hours and 45 minutes worth of media content into those daily 7½ hours" (2). In the early 2000s, David's multitasking might have seemed like another example of youthful media wizardry. A decade later, however, an observer might have been concerned about multitasking's negative effects on David's brain.

The popular story about multitasking has changed over the past two decades. Once attached to the computer's ability to perform parallel processing, multitasking became a buzzword describing what humans do with the power of technology. Corporate America embraced it as a vague job skill included in ads and résumés. As cell phones, handheld games, and video games became more sophisticated, the word became attached to youths' abilities. The word *multitasking* had and still conveys a sense of power, sounding scientific and mechanical. With *task* buried in the middle, the word exudes the sense of an important achievement. The word generates images of cell phones, shifting screens, and of connected, option-loaded lives. However, an alternate view emerged, largely through concerns over cell phones and distracted driving. Most recently, multitasking's distracting nature has been linked to its possible negative effects on how students focus on reading. The connected, option-loaded lives have become distracted, overloaded lives (Carr 2010; Rosen 2008). "The young are so good at multitasking" turned into "No one is very good at multitasking, and it's probably bad for us."

The scientific studies on multitasking seem resolute on this point: people generally don't do well when they do more than one task at a time or alternate between tasks (Dux et al. 2009). This general assessment has become part of the cultural conversation about technology use in the classroom, workplace, and home. However, multitasking isn't so simple as to deserve a blanket condemnation. One reason is the word *task*: not every task carries the same cognitive load. For instance, we can walk and talk without much difficulty because these tasks are routine; however, simultaneously reading a sentence and listening to a different sentence can be nearly impossible (Salvucci and Taatgen 2008, 101). The difficulty of each task influences the cognitive load, and the task's difficulty is influenced by purpose. We might assume that reading a celebrity gossip magazine while watching a sitcom would be less difficult than reading a science magazine while watching a complex drama; however, this assumption becomes complicated if the purpose of reading the gossip magazine is to rhetorically analyze it. We can speak in general terms about how good or bad people are at multitasking, but that does not serve us well when understanding situational, purpose-driven acts of literacy. Our teaching might be better served by realizing that not all multitasking is equal.

Why is this important? If we accept popular conceptions of attention and multitasking, instead of pursuing a more sophisticated understanding of the phenomenon, our perceptions of students' technology use may lead to ineffective pedagogy. Most of the scholarship on multitasking bears little relation to our concerns as teachers of reading and writing.[1] And most popular accounts of these studies conflate the many factors involved, leading to simple, generic conclusions that state "Multitasking is bad" or "Digital reading is less effective than print-based reading."[2] Composition's investigation into and increased awareness of multitasking is crucial in at least two regards. First, multimodal composition often entails the use of technologies—image editing programs, video software, audio software—that demand a high level of multitasking. My methods of teaching multimodal composition have been improved by the extra attention I've given to multitasking. Second, online reading is a daily experience for most students, and it's a growing part of teaching writing. I generally consider online reading to be a form of multitasking: hyperlinks within the text and within menus offer alternative tasks; pop-ups, animations, and videos redirect attention and purpose; and the web browser that surrounds the text is a complicated text in its own right, with navigational functions being the most obvious tasks.

By observing David's multitasking, I could tease apart some of the entangled factors within his multitasking and see their relationships. Before I saw his room, I had not planned on studying attention and multitasking. The exploratory nature of this study allowed me to adapt to the situation. Although what follows is nowhere near as precise as a planned study under laboratory conditions, it has the value of being closer to a real situation, with David's purposes for reading being his own. Out of all of the participants, David seemed to be the most comfortable, not changing much about his behavior because of my presence. Instead, as described in the opening scene, he continued various tasks. I took notes and audio-recorded the interview as I observed and asked questions about what he was doing. The home interview with David took over an hour, and he multitasked during all but ten minutes of it.

Reviewing the transcript and my notes, I isolated five significant factors in David's multitasking:

- Task: specific activity, includes purpose and context
- Tactic: reading strategy
- Text: message, includes the genre and medium
- Technology: device and interface used to access the text, includes search engines and other on-screen interfaces
- Training: experience and knowledge of the other four factors

Why these five? Each is essential to our concerns as teachers of reading and writing, especially with the inclusion of the reading tactic/strategy, which is a complex factor in studies of multitasking/hypertext reading (Salmeron et al. 2005). Also, I wanted to create a pedagogical heuristic that would be accurate but flexible. To break down and reduce each category further would turn the heuristic into a cumbersome checklist. This section is meant to be exploratory and suggestive, not exhaustive, of how these factors affected David's reading. From this observation, I have isolated two significant multitasking events, which I describe below with transcript excerpts.

In the first multitasking event, David switched between the online game *Fish Eat Fish* and eBay, where he was checking a bid status. *Fish Eat Fish* filled about one-third of the laptop screen. The game, which David explained to me as he played, was simple:

> *David:* It's a dumb little game, but it's fun. You play that little fish, and you have to eat the other fish and food pellets, which makes you bigger. The more you eat, the bigger you get. And the bigger fish eat you. Avoid them. And . . . that's about it.

> *Interviewer:* You play this a lot? You also play *World of Warcraft*, right?

> *David:* Yeah, like, this is really easy to play. And it doesn't matter if I lose. Like that. [His fish gets eaten; he has two lives left in the game. His next fish/life appears. He switches over to eBay, reads the screen, and switches back to *Fish* in about ten seconds. We both look to the top left corner of the screen to see whether he lost another life in the game while he was on eBay—he didn't. He resumes playing.]

> *Interviewer:* And *Warcraft* is more demanding. You can't flip between screens with that kind of playing.

> *David:* When I play that game [*Warcraft*], then I'm really play-ing that. You need to focus with that game. I play this when I don't care, if I have other stuff to do. See how big he gets? But I can't eat those bigger ones yet. [His fish still alive and much bigger now, David switches over to eBay and checks on his bid. He's back to the game within ten seconds.]

> *Interviewer:* How long on your bid? [I saw the screen, but didn't locate the information on it.]

> *David:* About ten minutes. I'm not going to get it, not at the rate others are bidding. Price is getting too high. I have some other bids on some car parts, but I have about thirty minutes and another hour on those.

In this event, which continued for seven more minutes, David switched between the text *Fish Eat Fish* and the text eBay. When switching to the *Fish* screen, his task was to locate his fish character, read the status of the character (the life and growth information on the top left and right of the screen, respec-tively), and to move the character with the arrow keys. The basic design of the game is similar to other video games, which bolstered David's familiarity with it. When switching to the eBay text, David's task was to figure out the time left and the current bid. David's tactic involved quickly scanning to locate the relevant information, sometimes hitting the refresh button if the information did not look current. These split-second readings and judgments impressed me because I had a hard time keeping up with David, who did it all seamlessly and never faltered during the conversation. Unfamiliar with both the game and eBay, I oriented less quickly with each screen change. David's extensive experience—his training—with the genres, the specific sites, and the interfaces enabled him to do this well. This observation gains more substance with the next event.

In this event, David's multitasking becomes more complicated. In addition to playing the game and checking bid updates, he looks up information on ESPN.com and a university webpage. He is still playing *Fish* while we discuss his view that he is a "bad reader":

> *David:* I don't know if I need tutoring on speed-reading or a better vocabulary, but I just don't . . . I'm not a good reader.
>
> *Interviewer:* What do your teachers say about your reading?
>
> *David:* You know. "I could do better." "Not working to my potential." That kind of thing. [David looks repeatedly at the silent ESPN on TV and then back at *Fish* during this.]
>
> *Interviewer:* Is it with all reading? That is, do you . . . ?
>
> *David:* Nah, just school reading. I don't do well on tests, and I don't always see the symbolism in English class. [David switches to ESPN.com and scans the information on the screen, which provides various game scores. Clicking for the scores to update takes about fifteen seconds. He then switches back to *Fish* and has to start over.]
>
> *Interviewer:* Do you go to that site [ESPN] often?
>
> *David:* Not much. Mainly just today. Been waiting for some baseball [scores], but they haven't been on TV, so I check sometimes. Anyway, I don't have a problem reading. I'm not dyslexic or anything like that. I just don't always get it.
>
> *Interviewer:* So, it's not that you can't get through the readings. You just don't understand them for class, for how you're expected to read them?

David: I get confused by Shakespeare. He . . . he confuses me. The way he wrote. Stuff like that. But if it looks even remotely, you know, like today's language, then I don't get confused. But I still don't see a lot of the hidden meanings. [David switches to ESPN.com and scrolls down the page, then back up the page, and clicks a Major League Baseball link. He scrolls down that page, but doesn't find the information, and returns to the *Fish* game. Seeing that his fish died, he switches to eBay, checks his bids, and then returns to his game. All of this switching and reading is fluid.]

Interviewer: I had trouble with some of the hidden meanings in English, too. [Long dialogue for two minutes. David continues to play the game, intermittently glancing at ESPN on TV and checking eBay bids. At one point, he finds the baseball scores on the ESPN.com. Then, he opens a window for the university website.]

David: Yeah, I hope college is different. If not, movies lied to me. [Laughs.] Okay, why . . . ? [David clicks on a "Financial Aid" link and slowly scrolls down the page, quickly scrolls to the top, and pauses before clicking a "Loans" link. Scrolls down. He looks at the screen for about a minute.]

Interviewer: What are you doing now?

David: I'm not sure I understood . . . [Reads the screen for another minute. Scrolls up, types "financial aid letter help" in the Search box. Scans the results. Returns to the main financial aid page.] That didn't help. I'll have to talk to . . . call somebody about that. [He switches to *Fish*, plays for about a minute, and then switches back to the financial aid page. He reads for about thirty seconds, clicks back to the main portal, and scans the available links. He gives up and returns to the game.] That's okay. I'll just call Monday.

Interviewer: Was that your first time visiting the school website?

David: No, I've gone there. Not much. It's hard to . . . that search engine sucks.

Interviewer: You don't visit the ESPN site much either. Why was it so easy to navigate?

David: [After a brief pause, he points at ESPN on TV.] Because it looks so much like the TV.

It did look like the TV. On SportsCenter, multiple windows of information floated around the center of the screen, scores of games rolled at the bottom of the screen (sometimes at the top), and text and graphics appeared and disappeared—the screen refreshed with new information and dissolved the old. The website and the TV screen resembled each other in numerous ways. It was reminiscent of Walter Ong's (1972) reflections on media interactions and transformations. He points to the possibility of "some paradoxical laws" in which a new medium does not "wipe out the old, but actually reinforces the older medium or media. However, in doing so it transforms the old, so that the old is no longer what it used to be" (405). Jay David Bolter and Richard Grusin (2000) would later describe such media transformations as *remediation*, a blurring of older and newer forms of media as they borrow from and refashion each other. This observation about remediation suggests even more complexity to Brandt's (1995) assertion that accumulation requires people to "piece together reading and writing experiences from more and more spheres, creating new and hybrid forms of literacy where once there might have been fewer and more circumscribed forms" (651). In one sense, if many, or even some, of those hybrid forms of literacy resemble each other through remediation, then perhaps some of the demanding nature of accumulation is alleviated. In this case, remediation helped to create a sense of familiarity for David as he navigated the ESPN website.

This familiarity happens more often than we consciously recognize, I think, because we like to imagine the web as a place of originality and creativity. However, when we easily navigate a new website, it's not only due to effective design, but also to remediation: we've seen something like it before. Most video sites resemble YouTube; most discussion forums resemble each other; people transitioned from MySpace to Facebook easily because each site uses similar templates. Kristin Arola (2010) observes that more of the web is moving toward this kind of easy design with the "rise of the template." She points to some troubling effects, including the concern that students may pay less critical and rhetorical attention to design issues. Arola has valid concerns, but template websites (like familiar genres) seem to make for easier reading by presenting information in familiar ways. With the accumulation of the number and kinds of texts, templates and familiarity help readers make sense of them more quickly. The "rise of the template" may also be driven by a culture of acceleration, with expectations of efficiency and speed being met through familiar reading and writing interfaces. Although David did not visit ESPN.com much, remediation added to his training, his storehouse of experience.

Rapidly switching between tasks, David was multitasking, and he handled it well. He probably would have performed better on the game had he not been switching to other tasks, but that misses the point: he chose the game because it was inconsequential, which reflects an awareness of priorities. He maintained ongoing concerns with eBay bids and baseball scores; with the former, he quickly discerned the rate of bidding would soon put the item beyond his price range. David stumbled with the university website because he lacked experience with the task and the text. Regarding the task, he didn't understand why he received less financial aid than expected; the vague nature of the problem and his fuzzy understanding of financial aid hampered his search. As a text, the website offered so much unrelated information that David felt overwhelmed. He did not know how to deploy reading tactics that would help him find the information, so he relied on skimming and scanning, and when he seemed to read in a more sustained way, he still did not find a solution. Also, in what I would consider a technological factor, he was unfamiliar with the university search engine, expecting it to be as helpful and easy to use as Google.

These multitasking events illustrate the importance of training and the value of teaching digital reading. David did well within the range of his usual experiences, but he struggled outside of that comfort zone; reading the university website was so cognitively challenging that his part of the conversation faltered for the first time. Assumptions that teens have a kind of all-encompassing digital expertise can lead to questionable pedagogies. I have fallen into this trap. For online research, I ask students to switch between multiple websites and to take notes on paper. When I assumed digital expertise among students,

I presented research strategies and examples without much context. Students got lost, especially when switching between sites. They didn't understand how to deploy strategies in certain situations, and failed to develop a systematic way to multitask for research purposes. Frustrated students and a bewildered teacher resulted from these experiences. I later realized I should have provided more details on how and why library websites and popular search engines work the way they do, especially in the students' specific research contexts. I also should have demonstrated how certain web browser functions could assist their research. Similarly, I have learned to incorporate more technical/functional aspects into multimodal pedagogy.

This teaching of functional literacy, Stuart Selber (2004) argues, is necessary in the digital age. Selber states literacy scholars are right to reject functional literacy as a basic set of skills divorced from social contexts. Not only is it bad pedagogy, but the simple view of literacy has tended to reinforce the "economic, cultural, and political status quo" (32). However, he argues that "to paint functional literacy with the broad brush of repression misses the fact that functional literacy is a necessary if not sufficient condition of all other forms of literacy" (33). Helping students understand and use technological resources can influence the uses of other literacies.

CONTROLLING SPEED AND DEPTH IN READING

David's multitasking is one lens on how attention is being used. Tim and Diana offer another interesting view of attention, especially in relation to the earlier discussion about the pedagogical value of slow, sustained reading. Most of the online reading they do involves skimming and scanning, mixed with some periods of more sustained reading. As they read in these ways, Tim and Diana performed the kinds of moves we want from composition students: reading for invention, analysis, evaluation, and synthesis.

These observations and interviews took place in Diana's home and Tim's home. With the home observations, I wanted to get a "lived-in" sense of their literacy practices. I hoped the participants would say more about their magazines, books, or computers if those literacy objects were nearby and that they would talk about their literacies differently when outside of the school environment. As I stated earlier, David was the only participant who seemed comfortable enough to continue his usual habits. Diana and Tim were less comfortable, each leading me to the dining room table for the same kind of interview we did in the school library.

Eventually, Tim led me through his house, talking about literacy objects—books in the living room, comic books stored in the basement, the computer in his room—and then demonstrating some of his online reading practices. Diana and I remained in the dining room, and she brought a laptop to the table. Diana and Tim demonstrated and described specific kinds of online reading, during which I asked questions, recorded audio, and took field notes.

Tim liked playing *World of Warcraft* (WOW). To him, the Massively Multiplayer Online Role-Playing Game (MMORPG) seemed as close as he could get to an interactive version of *Lord of the Rings*. He also enjoyed using paint programs to create images of characters for WOW and other MMORPGs. When Tim wanted to learn more, he visited WOW forum art threads and fantasy art forums, used Google image searches, and played the game (to study the game's art). In this research, Tim was "just getting a sense of what's out there, what other people do." When asked how long he normally spent on these sites, he responded: "Not long, but it depends. Some sites, less than a minute. But if I found cool examples, I would look at them—or interesting critiques—then I would look at that for a long time."

After Tim described his goals for this type of online reading, I asked about some of the specific websites and what he usually types into search engines, which then led to a demonstration on his computer.

> *Tim:* Well, I usually play the game for a while, but you probably don't want to see that. It sort of gets me in the right mood

and gets me thinking about the artwork. So, say I start paying attention to elves, then I'll do a search for elf art.

Interviewer: And how do you do that? What do you type? Are
there usual sites . . . ?

Tim: Um, yeah. [On Google, types "world warcraft elf art."]
That's just one way to do it. [Scans the search results.] Let's
see . . .

Interviewer: What are you thinking now? See anything interesting? And how do you—?

Tim: Like this Greywolf site is pretty cool. I've heard of that guy
[artist] before. [Clicks on the link, scans the webpage for
about one minute, looking at art and descriptions.]

Tim then explained that he saw some "awesome paladin art,"
which interested him, and "stuff like that sends me on another
search." After Tim found another gallery of paladin art, he
looked at the page and talked about the details of particular
images.

Interviewer: Do you take notes or anything while you're doing
this?

Tim: Not really, no. I kind of, like, let it sink in. I just take it in.
Same thing when I read people's critiques of *Warcraft* art. I
just take it in. Now, when I go to tip and advice sites about
how to do certain things with Photoshop, then I sometimes
take notes. In fact . . . [goes to Photoshop forum through
Google search, skims webpage.]

Interviewer: What are you doing now? This typical?

Tim: Yeah, I've seen some of this already. [Scrolls down page.]
Seen it. Seen it. [Scrolling down.] Yeah. Knew that stuff.

Interviewer: What happens when you see something new?

Tim explained he sometimes takes notes if the particular
advice is complicated and involves multiple steps: "I like doing
it while looking at the advice. Window open for the advice,
[another] window open for Photoshop. Then, I go through
the steps [from the advice forum.] I learn better by doing, and
I don't have much luck holding on to notes. They get lost."
Tim showed me some *World of Warcraft* art forums and pointed
out how detailed some of the responses were to art others had

posted. He did this while skimming and scrolling down the page; he said, "I can get fairly deep into this stuff when it gets detailed. I'll look at the art, then at the critiques, and then see what I think about it all."

Tim's reading was filled with stops and starts, with different speeds and depths. Within minutes, he could be skimming across the surface of several different websites, and then be locked onto one webpage, deep and focused. This kind of reading may not be unique to the web, but it's more likely to be a strategy with web reading. James Sosnoski (1999) argues as much when he describes the "hyper-reading" characteristic of "filtering," which involves selecting content that fits the reader's goals and experiences (165). Although filtering occurs with all reading, he points out that the "inordinate" scale of information we come across online leads to "a higher degree of selectivity than the print based, un-assisted reading we do away from our terminals" (167). When picking up a book, many cues help the reader determine whether it's worth reading—the cover, the table of contents, the index, the preface. The cues from the web—a brief title and two-line excerpt on a search page, a web address, the header and title of the site itself—are more difficult to make sense of quickly, especially when a Google search deposits the reader somewhere in the site, away from the home page and authorial information. Online we filter out more unnecessary, irrelevant information. Tim quickly read and dismissed some websites, slowed down for parts of others, and stopped when he came across something interesting or relevant.

This way of reading led to acts of invention for Tim. Sometimes the content of one website generated a research idea, which sent Tim to another website. Also, the details he saw in the art and the critiques contributed to his own artwork, giving him ideas he would not have otherwise had. He gathered useful ideas from slow and fast reading:

> Sometimes I slow way down if a critique is really thoughtful, but, you know, people can blather and ramble. At that point, I just start skipping through what they say, and I find some good things, some interesting ideas. They just need to edit. That guy!

[Stops scrolling. Points at screen, a long forum post.] Huge wall of words, man. I'm sure something's good in there, but he also probably likes to hear himself talk.

When I asked how he found interesting ideas from "skipping through what they say," Tim explained that certain words would indicate who was an experienced member of the community; these words were not set or predictable, but usually showed an extensive knowledge of the game or art, or both: "You just know when you see [the words]. They stand out." Tim's ability to recognize how "insiders" constructed themselves in this community would make him an insider of the community's discourse, even if he did not contribute that much to the community or read every discussion thoroughly.

Invention also occurred through his studying the discourse of the forum: "You've seen stupid people online, right?" Tim asked. "I don't want to be one of them, so I watch and see what others do. What gets good reactions? What makes you seem like a newb [short for newbie/novice]? Then, I know how to say things right." Tim noted he did not contribute that much to the forum, but he wanted to be respectful and careful when he did. He said he paid attention to how people "worded their criticisms in constructive ways" and how "much jargon they used." Although he was not interested in the social aspect of the community, Tim put significant thought into creating an effective ethos. From this rhetorical reading, Tim also gathered content ideas about what to critique and the kinds of suggestions to offer.

Although Diana read for different purposes, she used reading strategies similar to Tim's. Diana wasn't a news or political enthusiast, yet she tracked news stories across media: "I would go check my Yahoo! mail, and there would be news stories. I'd hear the news on the radio, then again at night on the [television] news." She noticed subtle differences in coverage, which inspired her to seek out different versions of news stories. Eventually, she visited specific news sites, but also searched for keywords from a news story to find other news sites covering the story. Some sites would cover a story more than others, and she gathered new keywords from these sites to find other examples of coverage. She did not actively seek the news story on radio or TV—"if it happens, great, but I'm not recording the news or anything"—but she checked the online versions of news magazines.

As we looked at her laptop, she opened up Yahoo! News and clicked on a random news article about the Iraq War. We both skimmed the article.

Interviewer: What now?

Diana: I might take the headline or some basic major words of the story and do a Google search. I don't know, I'll just type something [Google search for "Iraq War deaths." Scans the results.]

Interviewer: When you would look at these results, what do you look for?

Diana: Different headlines. Or if the brief description on Google makes it seem like it will be a different take [compared to the first version of the story]. So, this one [clicks on CNN.com] looks pretty long. If it were longer than the first one [on Yahoo!], then I would [scrolls down the page, highlights part of a paragraph] do that.

Interviewer: Ah, what are you . . . ?

Diana: That [highlighted] part is what's different [compared to the first story]. So, I copy some part of it and do a search on that.

[She then copied and pasted a part of the news article, searched for it on Google, and then scrolled down the page. She looked at the two-line descriptions of the Google hits. She clicked a few links and scrolled down them, reading quickly.]

Diana: And all of this looks the same. See, it all is like the original. Nothing really different.

Interviewer: And what if it did seem different?

Diana: Um, then I would think, what site is this? Is there a reason for the difference? You know, is the story really different now? I would read the whole thing [to look] for similarities and differences and what that would imply.

Interviewer: How do you know or decide when to click on a particular site that gives a different take on the story?

Diana: [Clicks back to Google.] Sometimes the title pages or descriptions on Google [result page] sound different than the first take. And then, I click the one that sounds different, and I just scroll down, looking for similarities and differences. When a difference pops up, then I stop and read.

Interviewer: And then what?

Diana: It depends. Let's go more in, see the later hits. [On Google search results, clicks the eighth page of results. Scrolls down. Points at web address.] See, that one is clearly a blogger. If he said something really interesting, I might Google that to see if anyone copied him, if he copied others, or anything like that. Just see where it goes. And it's not always, like, differences between websites. I've picked up on cable news leaving stuff out, really important information that makes a huge difference, and the news on the Internet will sometimes correct that.

Interviewer: Does the website point out that it's correcting the TV version?

Diana: Not really. I just piece it together. It's fun.

Like Tim's searches for fantasy art, Diana's news searches featured moments of skimming followed by sustained reading. Diana would quickly scan and exit some sites, and then slow down and focus on the next. She briefly did this slower reading in front of me, and she also explained how and when it usually happened.

Diana's reading was analytical and evaluative. She compared texts, examined differences, and sought to understand reasons for the differences. Until she talked about it with me, however, she did not appreciate or even recognize the complexity involved. The ways of reading demonstrated by Diana and Tim were far more complicated than the shallow skimming assumed by critics of online reading (Bauerlein 2008; Carr 2010). Indeed, Julie Coiro and Elizabeth Dobler's (2007) research on the online reading comprehension strategies of sixth-graders suggests an impressive degree of complexity to reading online. Coiro and Dobler state that achieving comprehension of Internet texts "may require readers to anticipate their understanding through multiple layers that are almost always hidden from view." The Internet reading in their study "seemed to demand many more attempts to infer, predict, and evaluate reading choices (e.g., hyperlinks followed) while anticipating the relevance of information in an open information space multiple levels beyond a visible link" (234). Although Coiro and Dobler offer a cautious note about how they did not compare the students' Internet reading to print reading, they point to the "possibility of a unique complexity to how skilled readers process Internet text compared to previous research on comprehending printed informational text" (234).

Also of interest to this study is Coiro and Dobler's argument that online reading seems to demand both faster and slower forms of reading:

> Skilled Internet readers must be able to regulate their movement between (a) newer online search and evaluation processes that typically occur very rapidly across hundreds of short Internet texts and (b) less spontaneous, more traditional self-regulation strategies within longer text passages that require more time and effort. These complexities, then, introduce a new metacognitive regulatory strategy required to combat the motivation of efficiency and spontaneity in order to ultimately slow down and read for meaning. (243)

Coiro and Dobler describe the choices of attention and speed that readers must make for different purposes. The view coming out of research is that teachers and students do not have to make a false choice of either fast or slow reading, but instead should develop ways of alternating between faster and slower forms of reading.

Tim and Diana enacted two complex forms of reading. The first I call *foraging*: a purposeful wandering across texts, evaluating and possibly gathering and using materials along the way. Diana gathered keywords and used them in future searches; Tim gathered art design ideas and references to websites to check out. The web, hyperlinked and multitask-ready, promotes this kind of connected reading in ways other media do not.

Certainly, TV shows, magazines, and books can inspire audiences to seek out other texts, but hyperlinks and an immediate search function make foraging far more likely on the web.

The second form of reading is a kind of oscillation between levels of depth and rates of speed. Diana and Tim each oscillated between different levels of depth: reading at shallow levels as they quickly skimmed and scanned the screen, sometimes skipping across the surface; and reading deeply, not necessarily the whole text, maybe just a fragment. They also oscillated between rates of speed: reading quickly, then slowly; fast reading followed by a focusing stop. When I asked Diana and Tim how they formed these reading practices, Diana gave a representative response: "But what should I be doing? What's the other choice? I guess I could get overwhelmed and stay off the Internet, or I could read everything, every word. But there's just so much out there, and this is how I do it." These forms of reading helped to manage information overload.

HYPER AND DEEP ATTENTION, FAST AND SLOW READING

What are we to make of the kinds of attention exhibited in this chapter? How can they inform a more robust sense of reading? Katherine Hayles (2007) provides a good starting point with her essay "Hyper and Deep Attention," in which she "explores the hypothesis that we are in the midst of a generational shift in cognitive styles that poses challenges to education at all levels, including colleges and universities" (187). The shift is from "deep" attention to "hyper" attention: deep attention is a single-object focus that is sustained; hyper attention, on the other hand, is characterized by desiring "multiple information streams" and having a "low tolerance for boredom" (187). Hayles does not malign one or hold another as an ideal. Instead, she recognizes situational advantages and disadvantages: "Deep attention is superb for solving complex problems represented in a single medium, but it comes at the price of environmental alertness and flexibility of response. Hyper attention excels at negotiating rapidly changing environments in which multiple foci compete for attention; its disadvantage is impatience with focusing for long periods on a noninteractive object such as a Victorian novel or complicated math problem" (188).

One advantage of Hayles' depiction of these cognitive styles is that she does not position *distraction* as the opposite of *deep attention*. In response to popular depictions of digital engagement as being "wired for distraction," Richard Miller (2010) wonders, "Am I splitting hairs to say that I see a difference between a state of distraction and mental wandering?" The distinction is accurate and useful. A distraction would involve switching focus to something unrelated to one's purpose; a mental wandering would be open to new ideas, possibly within the existing purpose or a new one. As the participants foraged through multiple sites and multiple texts, they encountered distractions, but did not give into negative distractions. The participants attended to multiple streams of information, shifting screens and texts with a sense of purpose and a dexterous handling of tasks. They were not getting lost in chains of hyperlinks, clicking away from one idea to a new, unrelated one. Online reading certainly has its share of distractions, but the relentless depiction of its "distracting nature" only serves to create images of people being constantly deterred from achieving anything, which is inaccurate and unhelpful.[3]

Hayles' (2007) distinction between "hyper" and "deep" attention can be useful, especially if perceived as a matter of degree and not a binary state; that is, hyper and deep may be best understood as polar ends on a continuum. I think the instances of oscillating by Diana and Tim show they are combining elements from each cognitive mode of reading. Especially impressive was how Diana, familiar enough with the genre and content of the texts she was reading, could drop in the middle of a website and read critically enough to see one news story's relation to other stories. Although participants engaged in hyper attention, they did not use it alone. The oscillation along that continuum may be more common than assumed. In his estimation of hyper and deep attention, John Guillory (2010) agrees with many of Hayles' assertions, but he points to a complication: "It is perhaps a mistake to see the mode of deep attention as oriented mainly toward the long work—that is, toward the question of the duration of attention. Poetry too, even short poems, demands sustained attention" (9). Deep attention may not require a long span of time. Rereading a short poem—a form of close reading—could be considered a kind of deep attention, but with a "slightly different cognitive and emotional experience with each reading." To Guillory, this example suggests "we will have to reconsider the relation between deep attention and close attention" (9). That is, the repeated, sustained attention on the brief poem is deep in its own way without the duration one might spend on a novel. One way to consider this relation is to see how Guillory's observation about short bursts of deep attention aligns with the observations I made of reading in this chapter: readers oscillate between hyper and deep modes of attention and faster and slower speeds of reading.[4]

As we move forward with more work on hyper and deep attention, we should incorporate other factors that influence attention with texts. Although Guillory (2010) and Hayles (2007) are certainly aware of other factors that shape reading, much of their discussion seems to focus on the kinds of attention "demanded" by certain texts. I understand the use of this shorthand, but if we are to better study attention and reading, we would benefit from considering the characteristics included in the heuristic—task, tactic, technology, text, and training—and examining how they apply with different people in different contexts, rather than assuming that the text is the only determiner of how something is read. For instance—to briefly consider a few of these characteristics—a novel (text) could be a complex piece, yet the context (task) and my training (experience) could result in a different level of engagement than assumed to read such a text. If I were in a reading group that valued talking about personal connection more than textual analysis, then I may choose to read less deeply at a faster rate, which my advanced training would help me to do quickly, but if I were to teach the text or write about it for publication, then I may choose closer, deeper attention and slower rates of reading for each context. In the previous chapter, we saw participants reading quickly (if at all) the school-assigned fiction that "demanded" deep, slow reading; they did this, at least in part, in recognition of the inconsistency of the speed-driven curriculum that asked them to read deeply.

In a culture of acceleration, it may be tempting for composition teachers to insist that school is a bulwark against the fast reading and the fast rhetorics employed by the participants. If students are already engaging in those literacies on their own, then perhaps it's our job to create a space for slow, careful reading. In *The Art of Slow Reading*, Thomas Newkirk (2012) makes a similar argument, positioning the "age of multitasking, of flitting from website to website" against the mindful, reflective, connective attention needed for slow reading; in urging slow reading, he wants us to be "present in our reading" (5–7). Newkirk anticipates that some will argue that his "advocacy for slowness is precisely the wrong advice for an age when students need the processing speed to handle so much information" (11). I would not make that exact argument; in fact, I agree that writing teachers should promote a deep, slow engagement with reading. And the six practices he offers in the book are thoughtful and effective methods for promoting that kind of engagement. Where I differ from Newkirk is in my argument that we should teach a range of reading speeds for a variety of purposes. We should help students learn to be mindful of when and how to employ a variety of reading strategies.

Various reading situations in and out of school will call for different forms of reading and attention. We can see this in the observations from this chapter. Given their situations and purposes, Diana, Tim, and David chose effective reading strategies. Diana had devised methods for recognizing quickly whether a webpage would be relevant for her current search; stopping to read every webpage from beginning to end would have been an unwise strategy. The need to strategize for different situations can also explain the "power browsing" used by people in a University College London (2007) study of online research habits. Both Carr (2010) and Newkirk (2012) cite the study, and Carr uses it as evidence that even academic researchers are not reading in the traditional sense when they go online (136–7). The study covered a range of researchers—from students to professors—who had access to journals, e-books, and other university resources, and found that everyone was "bouncing/ flicking" across sources and not reading completely: "Power browsing and viewing are the norm for all; reading appears to be undertaken only occasionally online, probably undertaken offline and possibly not done at all" (University College London 2007, 21). That last line is crucial because, although the study recognized that users downloaded and even printed research material, it did not examine what was done with the research after users logged off. That is, the users may have adopted more linear reading strategies when they read the downloaded materials. I am not assuming people were necessarily doing thorough research, but the general description of how people were skimming and power browsing does not sound unfamiliar or unreasonable. Considering the accumulation of research materials—both relevant and irrelevant—to sift through, skimming and power browsing seem like reasonable strategies for sorting and managing that much information.

In fact, I think back to how I performed research before the shift to online access, and realize a study of my strategies could have resulted in an alarming conclusion about the erosion of "traditional" reading. When researching, I would use the library database to locate several relevant books in the university library stacks. Once I physically located those books, I would also look on nearby shelves to find books with titles that seemed relevant. After acquiring a stack of books, I took measures to filter my choices, turning to the table of contents, the index, and the introduction. I flipped pages and scanned for particular keywords. Some books were discarded quickly, others remained longer, but most were put aside. Out of a stack of books, few were checked out and read. Much of that research experience sounds similar to the online "power browsing" described by the University College London study; in the library, I read little of the books, skimming and browsing to filter out and acquire the few materials that I needed. Instead of power browsing being a strategy unique to online research, it seems more likely that it is a reasonable response to the overabundance of research in general.[5]

Before concluding, it is worth pausing to examine Hayles' (2007) justification for the prominence of hyper attention. Hayles points to recent cognitive studies that reveal the brain as plastic, ever-changing and ever-responding, to argue that some young people's brains will be different from older people's: "plasticity implies that the brain's synaptic connections are coevolving with an environment in which media consumption is a dominant factor. Children growing up in media-rich environments literally have brains wired differently from those of people who did not come to maturity under that condition" (192). Hayles is not alone in her concern about the effects of prolonged technology use.

Hayles (2007), Carr (2010), and numerous popular arguments raise concerns about media exposure that seem overstated, and they trouble me as a teacher. For instance, starting at the level of representation, the metaphor of students' brains being "wired differently" seems to pathologize technology use and student behavior: "Why aren't students reading books? Because texting and video games rewired their brains!" At the same time that these critics point to the brain's plasticity, the "wired" image sounds "hardwired," locked and unchanging due to media's power. "Wired" also creates a mechanistic image of the brain that mirrors the gadgets in youths' hands. When I come across fears of brains being "wired differently" in numerous accounts, I get the sense of two possible wiring patterns, the "normal," book-based wiring, and the "different," digital-based wiring.[6] In this sense, the effects of technology also sound deterministic: increased media exposure (and that alone) will rewire brains differently from the "normal" wiring, which assumes all media exposure besides books will rewire the brain in a similar direction/pattern. Thus, we teachers will have one kind of brain, and students will have another kind of brain. If we embrace the metaphor (or thoughtlessly adopt it) as teachers, it may only create a further sense of distance and difference between teachers and students.

The concern that extensive multitasking and prolonged web reading will undermine complex thinking also seems overstated. The evidence for brains being "wired differently" comes largely from scans of brains under various conditions. It's important to note that brain scans from functional magnetic resonance imaging (fMRI) experiments capture only snapshots of the brain under certain conditions (often simple conditions due to the constrained environment of the MRI machine); the experiment's stimulus leads to neural activity, which then causes blood to rush to the related, active parts of the brain, which causes a small change in the magnetic field (from the iron in the blood). Such scans can suggest what may be occurring in parts of the brain at the time, but issues of cause-and-effect and long-term effects are much harder to determine. In their review of neuroscience research on reading, George Hruby and Usha Goswami (2011) observe that, despite the increasing number of studies, "the majority of imaging findings are less than a decade old and are thus unreplicated. Meta-analyses are scarce" (167). Devising pedagogical responses at such an early stage of research would be unwise.

I don't mean to minimize what cognitive neuroscientists do; rather, I caution non-experts against drawing conclusions about technology's effects on literacy practices from such studies, especially when they are reported in popular news accounts. Non-experts have a tendency to fall for the "seductive allure" of neuroscience (Weisberg et al. 2008), a tendency encouraged by popular news stories, which oversimplify and overemphasize neuroscience results. In one study of reactions to neuroscience, people tended to rank the credibility of brain research higher if it included brain scan images (McCabe and Castel 2008); another study showed that the words "brain scans indicate" made the explanation of brain activity sound more convincing to those with little or some knowledge of neuroscience (Weisberg et al. 2008). Rhetorician Jordynn Jack and neuroscientist L. Gregory Appelbaum (2010) advise readers outside of the neuroscience field "to be careful about applying scientific results to new contexts, such as rhetorical ones" (427); the same warning should apply to literacy education contexts as well.

Technology certainly influences how we read and think. But, as argued in chapter three, technology does not do this alone, and speed-driven technologies are a part of a speed-driven culture. Technologies are not isolated and neutral, but linked to a combination of institutional, social, cultural, and political forces that shape their use. We might be wise to hesitate before attributing a perceived "hyper attention" to the effects of interactive media alone.

NOTES

1   For instance, one study compared how well heavy multitaskers and light multitaskers focused under different conditions, with participants from each group trying to recall whether red rectangles on a screen had changed position after distracting information—blue rectangles—had been introduced. The tasks and the time differences between the multitaskers' successes were measured in milliseconds (Ophir, Nass, and Wagner 2009). The light multitaskers were better at filtering the distracting information. If I were to extend such a study to the classroom, the result would be a simple, and possibly misleading, message: students who regularly multitask often get distracted easily. Let me be clear: I am not criticizing the ultimate value of such studies. Most are simply asking disciplinary questions different from those of interest to literacy scholars.

2   Carr (2010) cites hypertext reading studies to illustrate the inherent distraction of the hyperlink. Without giving a full rebuttal, I think a few things should be kept in mind with respect to Carr's claims. At least two of the studies he describes are problematic as evidence: they asked participants to read hypertext fiction (an unfamiliar genre), and in one of the studies, a linear story was turned into hypertext with random links. Other studies measured effective hypertext reading in various ways – comprehension, memory, and navigation. Carr wants to turn all of these studies into a generalization about the web: "It presents information not in a carefully balanced way but as a concentration-fragmenting mishmash" (131). In their review of fifteen years of hypertext research, Salmeron et al. (2005) acknowledge uneven results about hypertext reading, but they note that reading strategies have not been controlled for in many studies.

3   More studies are complicating this general claim that multitasking is necessarily distracting. For instance, R. Kelly Garrett and James Danziger (2007) examined the use of instant messaging (IM) in the workplace

through a survey of 912 workers who use computers. The authors found that those who used IM reported more computer-mediated communications but fewer interruptions than those who did not use IM. This finding of more communication but reduced interruption seems counterintuitive. However, as the authors argue, what is most likely happening with the IM users is that they have created "communication practices that minimize some types of interruption and negotiate the timing of others." The workers use IM to "engage in briefer, more frequent interactions in order to get quick answers to work-related questions with minimal disruption, to participate in loose, flexible collaboration, and to coordinate more intense interactions to protect time on task for higher-order activities" (36).

4   This oscillation of attention and speed seems true for most reading. Even the deep attention devoted to a long, complex novel might fade in and out, with closer focus at times giving way to a more casual engagement. Readers might linger over some words and move quickly past others. Of course, as I explain in the chapter, purpose and experience influence reading strategies. Studies of expert readers show them engaging in "selective attention," slowing down to focus on certain parts, but also knowing when to skim (Pressley 2002; Zhang and Duke 2008). Experienced scientists read journal articles nonlinearly and selectively; their strategies "reflect the small amount of time scientists have (or make) available for reading; like any other professionals, they rarely can devote attention to work that is irrelevant to their immediate purpose or their general research program" (Charney 1993, 212).

5   The history of reading suggests "traditional" reading is complicated by a range of strategies used by different readers at different times. The "power browsing" noted in the library study may be a variation of a long-used strategy. As historian Ann Blair (2003) observes, "Many of the methods for managing an abundance of texts have remained identifiable in one form or another from antiquity to the present day: they typically involve selecting, sorting, and storing, carried out in various combinations and with various motives and technologies" (12). I noted in chapter three that we should not reduce all historical examples to a relative sameness; specifics matter in regard to context, particularly the purposes and technologies that influence the reading. Blair recognizes the need for contextual details, and she also proposes it is "safer" to "assume that in most periods proficient readers have deployed a range of different kinds of reading in different circumstances" (13).

6   An article from *The New York Times* (Richtel 2010) is a good example of the concern over youths' brains being "wired differently." In the article, Michael Rich, associate professor at Harvard Medical School, states of youths' multitasking: "Their brains are rewarded not for staying on task but for jumping to the next thing." If the effects of such "rewards" persist, Rich argues, then brains will change: "The worry is we're raising a generation of kids in front of screens whose brains are going to be wired differently" (Richtel 2010). The article's title is suggestive as well: "Growing Up Digital, Wired for Distraction."

5

READING-WRITING CONNECTIONS

*"This is one literal way that many of us read now, from
the position of the writer, with our hands on keypads and
through the same material mediums through which we write."*
– Deborah Brandt (2009, 166)

Julia once again took time after school to talk to me about the high school, her students, and her teaching experiences. As she moved stacks of student papers on her desk, one stack tumbled and sheets fanned out, black print on white paper. Scanning the fallen stack, I saw the usual: essays about Shakespeare and Hemingway, reports and proposals and analyses. Amidst some business proposal assignments, I saw a page with color and graphics.

Noting my interest, Julia handed the proposal to me. "That's great, isn't it? I think she's proposing a nightclub for teenagers in that."

The proposal showed a graphic design of the nightclub's name and included the incorporation of Google maps. The student used the maps to help argue for the club's location, with different maps offering perspectives on the location scattered between the text.

"This is wonderful. Were students asked to use images?"

"No. She just did that on her own. A few other kids did something like that, too."

"Did you look at models in class that showed them how to do this?"

"No," Julia said. "They must be reading stuff like that on the Internet."

Julia explained that the additional visual elements did not harm the students' grades, but they did not help either. Although

DOI: 10.7330/9780874219333.c005

Julia appreciated the students' visual creativity, the curriculum did not have a mechanism for rewarding or encouraging it. Julia and I discussed our experiences with students who attempted to bring out-of-school literacy practices into school, and we wondered how many students considered crossing such boundaries but did not take the risk.

In an interview in the school library, and in response to a question about the kinds of writing she did at home, Lauren mentioned she was one of the students who added visuals to the business proposal assignment. She said she added the visuals "partially out of boredom, but also because it seemed right to do. It made sense." When I asked why, she explained:

> A lot of reasons. You see movies, and some guy is making a presentation in a business room with PowerPoint and pictures to back up what he's trying to sell. The pictures can't simply be pretty or cool. They have to add something. And when I sometimes make invitations to events and things and invite people, I started using Google [Maps] images. I need landmarks when I'm trying to find a place, so why not show instead of tell? Yeah, the step-by-step directions are great, and you can write [additional directions], but the map helps out faster, I think. But I didn't start it. I forget what [another student] was trying to propose in his, but he was the one who got others to do it. He started it, and he put, like, real images from Google in his, and then a few of us thought [of] Google Maps.

Two parts of Lauren's explanation speak to the concerns of this book. First, for Lauren, changing what was expected of her writing made sense based on the writing she did at home and saw in media representations. Apparently, other students had the same attitude as Lauren regarding the adaptations they made to the assignment. Second, she had developed a conscious rhetoric for visuals, recognizing they "can't simply be pretty or cool. They have to add something." Part of this recognition came from her experiences making invitations for friends and incorporating Google Maps images. However, she was not only thinking critically about how to use images, but also how to use them in relation to words. Lauren was thinking about the capabilities and limitations—the affordances—of each mode of communication in this particular situation (Kress 2003). As Julia observed, Lauren and her classmates did not study models for this in school: "They must be reading stuff like that on the Internet."

This chapter turns to the reading-writing relationship and considers how the web provides models of reading and writing. The web as a provider of models stems from two important features: the web's capacity for spreading information and its role in social networking. The accumulation of literacy noted by Deborah Brandt (1995) is amplified by the web: genres and media pile up and spread out in cyberspace. This proliferation allows readers and writers to pursue interests and join groups that might have been otherwise unavailable to them. In this regard, models of writing are there to be examined, imitated, and learned by would-be writers. What helps the models to flourish, though, is the social aspect of the web, which promotes interaction among people with similar interests; they gather around these genres and media and help each other do things with them. In this chapter, I examine the role of such social interactions as they affect two participants' experiences of reading-to-write in online environments, and consider how the reading-writing relationship has changed in an age of accumulation and acceleration. To set the context for my examination of how the web promotes and assists writing, however, I explore the participants' perceptions of reading-writing connections in college.

READING AND WRITING IN COLLEGE

David, Tim, Diana, and Amy had first-year university experiences that, in academic terms, were easy in some regards and frustrating in others. Amy, David, and Tim stayed near home, with David and Tim attending the same public university while Amy attended a private university. Diana traveled across the state to another public university. Emotionally and socially, they experienced great change: friends moved and faded away, and they left the comfort of home for lives in dorms and apartments. I met with Amy, David, and Tim on campus for this portion of the study and also communicated with them via e-mail; Diana and I communicated over e-mail. When we talked about their academic experiences, they spoke of being alternately bored and overwhelmed. With orientations and student mentors, they came to a better understanding of campus culture, but the culture of the classroom remained a mystery. As high school seniors, most knew how to "game" the system as described in chapter three, reading in tactical ways to manage the workload. Some also seemed comfortable experimenting with writing during their senior year, most likely because of the relatively small risk involved.

The fullness of each student's entry into college is beyond the scope of this book's argument. I will focus this section on how two students struggled with a similar problem of college reading-writing. A self-described "bad reader" of print texts in high school, David continued to struggle in college. We usually met in a quiet space of the library or communicated via e-mail. During each interview, I asked general questions about adjusting to college life and then moved to more specific questions about reading and writing. He said his college English classes were easier than his high school English classes "on most days. You don't have the same pace as in high school." But he found essay assignments confusing and "didn't know what the teacher wanted." He showed me writing assignment directions, which I interpreted for him a few times. Although the directions seemed clear to me, I also recognized all of the unspoken assumptions that eluded David. I elaborated on directions to "analyze" and "provide arguments and evidence for your thesis," which led to the kind of teacher-student conference interactions I have with my own students. I asked David, "How do you talk about reading and writing in class?" He responded that they talk "about what we thought about the stuff we read" and that students "get into groups often." He did not have a clear sense of how the readings led to or complemented the writings in the course:

> I thought we were reading to get exposed to different viewpoints and cultures. Just to get more experience reading. The writing we do is really different. And the teacher doesn't really go over the writing the way you did. Maybe I'm just really behind on what

all of that [the directions] is supposed to mean. And the readings—nothing "sinks in" with them. I read them, but they don't make sense. I can tell you what they're about—kind of—but not much after that. I know this isn't a great answer. Some students play along well, and they get into the arguments about cultural issues, but I don't get it.

We tried to talk about the readings—a mixture of fiction and non-fiction with which I had some familiarity—and David had a sense of a reading's gist, but not the particulars or how he constructed the meaning as a reader. When I asked David about reading in other classes, he said the experience was similar to the reading he did in high school:

> I don't know. I can't think of how it's any different from high school. We have textbooks. Chapters get assigned. I barely read them. Feels pretty much the same. We don't talk about the textbooks, and it seems like the notes from lectures will give you what you need from the books, so there isn't much reason to read them all the way through. It's just stuff to do, work to keep you busy, I think.

I directed the conversation back to his English class and inquired whether he had any sense that the class was preparing him for reading and writing in other classes. He said, "It might be. I think all the teachers do a good job. I'm not a great reader, and I'm sure I could work harder at that. But I have a hard time doing that [working harder] when I can't even figure out where to start with the homework."

From this discussion, I was reminded of the students who struggle with reading in my first-year writing classes. They brush past entire passages and ideas, disregarding them as they come across and grasp a few ideas that seem familiar, that they can do something with—connect to previous knowledge, a personal experience, a cultural argument. At the time, as a researcher who started to feel like an advocate for David's education, I blamed the teacher for not providing clearer writing assignments or offering a more engaging, sophisticated reading pedagogy. Yet as a writing teacher who knew the frustrating experience of providing instructions that all but a few students understood, I also wondered whether I should sympathize with the teacher. For the purposes of this research, however, I was more interested in how the students understood their transition between high school and college literacy practices and how they perceived the reading-writing relationship in their classes; I was less interested in examining the specific pedagogies of the teachers. In this case, David did not see any real connection between reading and writing, and he had no models to turn to for his writing.

Diana attended a public university over an hour away from her hometown, and we communicated via e-mail. An astute reader and general overachiever, she placed out of the first-year composition course. She took on demanding courses, which suited her experience and personality. In the early weeks of college, she claimed to move between disciplinary expectations of reading and writing without many problems. She could not describe how she did this, explaining her actions in terms of adapting to teachers' expectations: "You just have to figure out what [teachers] want. It's pretty simple." She did not seem to have a metacognitive awareness of how she adapted as a reader in these situations, which may have been a stumbling block when she could not "figure out" teachers' expectations. Diana then found her usual ways of reading did not work anymore, noting "they [teachers] expect us to do different things in different classes with reading. And the contradictions don't make sense to me."

Although Diana maintained good grades, she felt frustrated by expectations among teachers that grew increasingly divergent. In particular, teachers' different rules for research "are strange. My [literature] teacher tells us to use many sources. Movies, websites, essays, even blogs. My history teacher? He actually said, 'If I see an Internet source on your paper, it will automatically fail.'" Diana eventually navigated these expectations, revising the literature paper "because my writing wasn't good enough in an early draft. In particular, how and why to put research in was a big problem for me. I ended up buying a research book off Amazon." The history essay was "just awful.

But I did it, and I think the exams will make up for [the grade on the paper]." She had written research papers in high school, but Diana did not understand the logic behind research in college: "I feel like I'm guessing a lot."

I want to emphasize how David and Diana—two very different students in terms of self-confidence and academic reading proficiency—struggled with navigating the shifting forms and unclear expectations for reading and writing in college, which is not uncommon (Carroll 2002). Indeed, I see these experiences every year with a range of first-year composition students. In the context of this chapter's focus on reading-writing connections, it is possible both Diana and David would have been helped by being given not only clearer directions, but also a clearer sense of the articulations between reading and writing, including models for their writing.

IMITATION AND THE RELATIONSHIP BETWEEN READING AND WRITING

Composition has had an uneasy relationship with imitation. Noting the elusive nature of the term *imitation*, Frank Farmer and Phillip Arrington (1993) offer the following "working definition": "*the approximation, whether conscious or unconscious, of exemplary models, whether textual, behavioral, or human, for the expressed goal of improved student writing*" (13, italics original). Farmer and Arrington note the long rhetorical tradition of imitation, but observe that, by the 1990s, there had been, among the composition community, a "largely *tacit* rejection of imitation" (12, italics original). The sources of that rejection most likely stemmed from the process movement: emphases on invention and on process over product might have caused some teachers to regard imitation as a copy of a product—a step in the wrong direction. Indeed, in the early 1970s, Edward Corbett (1971) and Frank J. D'Angelo (1973) listed precisely those reasons as they argued for the use of imitation. Corbett states there is "no question" that students learn through imitation, yet the "present mood of education theorists is against such structured, fettered training. The emphasis now is on creativity, self-expression, individuality" (249). According to D'Angelo, some teachers regarded invention as original, creative, and the opposite of imitation, which was seen as "counterfeiting, tracing, and stereotyping" (283). In addition to these objections to imitation, its connection to reading most likely did not help. To imitate well means paying close attention to what other writers do, studying their choices and the effects of those choices: Why did the writer choose that syntax, that word, that punctuation mark? Such attention to reading might have also conflicted with the desired emphasis on the student's self-expression and creativity.

I can understand some teachers' reluctance to use imitation. Imitation raises questions about some of the foundations of composition. Although composition teachers generally recognize that "original" and "the individual writer" are fraught concepts, we still expect students to produce individualized and original work (Bakhtin 1981; Porter 1986). Supplying models to study and imitate further complicates this expectation. Another foundational concept of composition involves leading students through a process, not providing them a formula for producing a particular kind of text. This concept leads to pedagogical challenges every step of the way, from constructing an assignment to giving revision feedback: teachers must be specific without providing a step-by-step map. However, this emphasis on process over product can transform pedagogy that respects writing's complexity into a pedagogy that unwittingly reinforces writing's mystery. That is, some students flourish with mild suggestions and half-fixes, and others remain baffled by academic rules and expectations. Lisa Delpit (1995) argues that teachers should not ignore the importance of the product and that some students could benefit from clearer articulations of academic discourse rules. Too heavy a focus on process can "create situations in which students ultimately find themselves held accountable for knowing a set of rules about which no one has ever directly informed them" (31).

Imitation offers other benefits as well. Imitation engages students in a different kind of reading than they are often accustomed to, one that requires an active, playful interaction with the text. It also creates an opportunity to examine and evaluate another writer's ability, but not in a way that makes such writing seem unattainable. Through these other benefits, students can also become more confident and capable readers and writers. In recent years, scholars have made strong arguments for imitation (Butler 2008; T.R. Johnson 2003), and with the success of Gerald Graff and Cathy Birkenstein's (2006) *They Say / I Say*, which provides discourse templates for students to imitate, composition may be on the verge of a wealth of new scholarship and pedagogy in this area, crafting a new relationship with imitation.

Imitation, with its inherent tensions between originality and direct instruction, is one manifestation of the sometimes uneasy relationship between reading and writing. Deborah Brandt (2009) describes another form of discord when she argues that writing is beginning to overtake reading: "For perhaps the first time in the history of mass literacy, writing seems to be eclipsing reading as the literate experience of consequence" (161). Brandt reflects on the reading-writing relationship, noting that writing and reading obviously cannot happen without the other, but this connection does not mean that conflicts do not exist; she states we "have spent less time thinking about how reading and writing can be in competition with each other, how they can be antagonistic to one another, how the uses and practices that grow up around the one might challenge and change the other" (162). Brandt suggests that, in this new relationship shaped by globally networked economies, "reading is being undone by writing—at least as reading has been traditionally understood" (162). Brandt locates two significant shifts in this "undoing" of traditional reading. First, there is the shifting of values in literacy, from mass reading's moral ties (Graff 1987) to mass writing's connections with work and product; it is here that the "heritage of reading is being undermined by the heritage of writing" (Brandt 2009, 162). The second shift has occurred in the repositioning of readers, who are increasingly reading from a writing position, with the two acts "almost indistinguishable from one another" (166). Much of Brandt's argument comes from her studies of workplace writing, and she provides compelling evidence for this aspect of the shifting reading-writing relationship.

I do not dispute the shifts identified by Brandt. However, I argue that, in other environments, the reading-writing relationship is more cooperative than conflicting, and a different economic frame is at work. Brandt's (2009) economic frame for the relationship centers on the workplace, and she examines writing for its "commercial or transactional value" (164). However, I think a different shifting of the reading-writing relationship has occurred in some online writing environments, many of which provide explicit models and assistance with writing. This shift marks a cooperative aspect to the reading-writing relationship. The reading, writing, and mentoring occurring in these spaces take on an economic quality based more on social and cultural capital than on monetary capital. As James Porter (2010) has argued, all writing "resides in economic systems of value, exchange, and capital." Porter observes that money may be involved, but "the motivation could just as easily be based on desire, participation, sharing, emotional connectedness" (176). Collective participation and a shared sense of responsibility are features of many online spaces. One of the most popular sites of collective reading-writing is Wikipedia, the non-profit encyclopedia with volunteer editors. In no small way do the Wikipedia editors maintain a consistency of format and tone, following a model of how an entry should look and sound, and working collaboratively to create new models when needed.

Media scholar Henry Jenkins (2008) provides another example of this cooperative reading-writing relationship from fan fiction forums. He describes fourteen-year-old Heather Lawver and how she started *The Daily Prophet*, an online newspaper set in the world of *Harry Potter*. Lawver's site attracted hundreds of young international contributors who wrote news stories about characters from the series. She served as Chief Editor, attending to each submission to prepare it for publication. Lawver described the *Prophet*'s purpose to the parents of the contributors in this way:

By creating an online "newspaper" with articles that lead the readers to believe this fanciful world of *Harry Potter* to be real, this opens the mind to exploring books, diving into the characters, and analyzing great literature. By developing the mental ability to analyze the written word at a young age, children will find a love for reading unlike any other. By creating this faux world we are learning, creating, and enjoying ourselves in a friendly utopian society. (Jenkins 2008, 179–80)

As Jenkins observes, "Lawver is so good at mimicking teacherly language that one forgets that she has not yet reached adulthood" (180). Indeed, Lawver even developed detailed plans for teachers to create versions of the newspaper as classroom projects. Given the elaborate writing produced for the newspaper, it is not surprising that teachers followed Lawver's model.

Although Lawver's accomplishment of being a writing tutor/ teacher at such a young age is remarkable, I want to emphasize two significant elements of this reading-writing example. First, Lawver encouraged contributors to read the published examples as models for their own submissions. Second, the writers did not merely write for their own sake, producing fan fiction that could have been submitted to any website. Their writings were shaped around the website's particular design; they read models, read each other's work, and wrote to maintain a shared vision of the site. Contributors created personas that existed within the Potter world, often describing themselves as friends or relatives of popular characters. The personas were detailed and became part of other contributors' writings in what became a collaborative effort to expand the narrative: "The result is a jointly produced fantasy—somewhere between a role-playing game and fan fiction. The intertwining of fantasies becomes a key element of bonding for these kids, who come to care about one another through interacting with these fictional personas" (Jenkins 2008, 184–85).[1] The *Prophet* writers followed the design of the site, drawing on the resources of the site to make their own contributions. In such a space, the economic exchange involves free labor and social capital; reading and writing are joined in cooperation, not competition. Contributors gained the opportunity to practice writing in a safe, mostly pseudonymous space and were able "to feel like an expert while tapping the expertise of others" (186). The *Prophet* is just one of hundreds of fan fiction forums. As of 2011, FanFiction.Net, the largest fan fiction forum, had over 5,000 story categories and over three million submitted stories (Sendlor 2011).

As the examples of Wikipedia and *The Prophet* demonstrate, the web is a prominent space in which writers imitate the texts they read. I attribute this prominence to accumulation, acceleration, and the "social turn" of Web 2.0. Various genres accumulate on the web; they pile up and spread out across a vast, ever-growing digital space. We access and navigate more genres than ever before. Speed is also a key element to this access. We can load multiple sites, multiple texts with minimal delay, and we can move quickly between these texts through tabbed browsing. The social aspect of the web encourages participation and feedback. Robert Cummings (2009) comments on the appeal of this sense of immediate communication: "The immediacy of Internet chat allows participants to cycle through the roles of writer and reader, thereby accounting for some of that medium's popularity with student writers. Students who write in wikis cite some of these same reasons for an intense involvement with their text: they know that what they submit to a group collaboration document will be quickly—if not immediately—assessed and edited by other readers" (14). When reading online, we come across a range of writers, from amateur to professional, who provide models; when writing online, we have faster access to audiences and feedback.

Of course, people were inspired by and imitated other writers before the web. Fan fiction, a popular genre online, did not originate with the Internet. For instance, fans of the original *Star Trek* television show wrote stories that imagined alternative storylines for characters and kept the show's universe alive after the show was cancelled.[2] Clearly, this kind of writing is not new. Many people have been inspired to write by a favorite novelist or poet. However, I think online reading and writing offer new tools and opportunities for imitation. One reason is obvious: when reading a book, people often do not have a pen or any other writing tool at hand; they are not reading from the position of a potential writer. Computers, on the other hand, put people in the position of both reader and writer, not only with the keyboard, but also with copy and paste tools that allow easy appropriation. This ability to switch between the position of a reader and the position of a writer is a significant shift in the reading-writing relationship. Cummings (2009) sees this shifting of reading-writing positions as central to wiki writing: "This event—the crossing of role boundaries between reader and author—is such a fundamental aspect of the wiki writing environment that it becomes its dominant characteristic" (15). The tools, the speed, the convenience—these are key factors that promote this change. People also get to see other amateur writers online, and this sparks the realization that someone does not have to be a published professional to write. A favorite novelist or poet can inspire someone to write, but can just as easily intimidate a reader into not writing. Finally, people can become a part of a reading-writing community that offers a safe space in which to take risks.

All of these features of online reading-writing forums can provide reader-writers with resources and motivation to successfully imitate in the service of producing new texts. The social components of such sites extend and enrich the benefits rhetoricians have long attributed to imitation, and at least some contributors to these sites engage in the kinds of careful reading and writing—including paying attention to genre and audience—that we encourage in the composition classroom. However, as the interview excerpts below reveal, study participants often had more difficulty identifying opportunities for imitation in their assigned reading and writing than they did in their out-of-school literacy practices.

READING-WRITING FAN FICTION

Tim preferred to multitask when I interviewed him at his university campus. As I asked him questions about college reading and writing experiences, we walked through the library aisles, and he picked up books he needed to write his research papers. The gathering of books halted as Tim told stories about his classes; then we would move on to collect the next book. The stories would be intermittently interrupted by talk about the book and the research in front of him. He openly admitted to feeling nervous about the rigorous demands of college, and he seemed to appreciate the opportunity to vent to a teacher-researcher. As we walked among the rows of books, Tim said he loved college, but felt adrift when it came to expectations for his writing:

> The college experience itself is great. I don't feel prepared for the actual work, though, which is fairly distressing, you know? I mean, look at this book. And these books [in his hands]. I have to do a research paper on this topic, and I don't know what to do once I check them out. I'll read them, yeah, and find quotes to put in the paper, but I don't know what's really going on with it. It's going to be some bad writing—ideas all over the place. I'll make some sense of it. Maybe I'll do okay [on the paper]. But right now I have no idea what I'm doing.

As with David, I talked about the assignments with Tim when he seemed open to that kind of exchange. And his problems with school reading and writing echoed those experienced by David and Diana. Tim found ways to "fake the [research] paper" and did not see it as a learning experience. He said, "I don't know what it's supposed to look like—except not a report, like we did in high school—and I don't know what I'm getting out of writing it. Feels like there's a secret handshake that I didn't get."

After two interviews, Tim mentioned he no longer created art for the online game *World of Warcraft* (see chapter four); instead, he wrote stories and submitted them to fantasy fiction forums:

> I know. Big leap, right? But it really is, I think. It's still very geeky. I'm aware of this. I like to write now, at least for this. It was hard to get used to at first, knowing where to go on the site and how to get started. Once you do, though, the being anonymous is fantastic. You can start clean, fresh. Be anyone you want. And that's part of what makes it easy—you can look stupid and no one knows. That sounds great to me. That's a refreshing outlet for me.

Tim's appreciation of being able to "start clean" was interesting, particularly when put into the context of his tendency in high school to read the assigned novels his friends were reading in the year ahead of him, which offered him a safe space for his interpretations. I do not think his using this site was only in reaction to his frustrations with coursework, but he mentioned several times how the website, the fiction he wrote, and the anonymous interactions with others were a form of escape. Sitting in the library's open computer lab, Tim logged into a *Lord of the Rings* fan fiction site:

> *Tim:* It's comforting. [Points at the screen.] Like when I get into a really good book, but I'm a character. Stormbringer [his login name]. Yeah. Don't laugh.

> *Interviewer:* Stormbringer is your name in the site, right? That's the name other writers use to address you. It isn't a character?

> *Tim:* Yeah. It's a goofy name I picked on the spot for me as a writer. I wasn't sure I was going to stick around until I read some of the writing, which was pretty good. Compared to how I've been writing lately—it was cool to see people knowing what they were doing.

> *Interviewer:* Your fiction writing? Your academic writing? Which were you not happy with?

> *Tim:* School writing. I didn't start writing [fiction] until this site. The writers were friendly and helpful to others in feedback. And they all seemed so confident—but humble, laid-back—with what they knew about writing and writing fantasy fiction.

Tim's descriptions of the forum writers not only signaled the pleasure of "escape," but also the quality of the writers, which included—but was not limited to—their actual writing. Tim enjoyed the quality of their writing, but pointed to other aspects of their online presence: "They're not professionals, but they're good. I enjoy just reading them, especially when they're awesome and get me lost in their words. And they make guys like me think I can do it, too." He admired the writers because "they all seemed so confident" and "friendly." These qualities helped draw Tim into the site and supported his attempt at writing fiction. As Robert Brooke (1988) argues, an important element of successful imitation is that it involves a person, not a text: "Writers learn to write by imitating other writers, by trying to act like writers they respect. The forms, the processes, the texts are in themselves less important as models to be imitated than the personalities, or identities, of the writers who produce them" (23). Taking on an identity in regard to writing means "taking a stance towards experience, towards reading, towards writing. It involves taking on a particular identity, a way of being a certain person in the social world" (38).

I want to unearth the aspect of "reading" from Brooke's statement and point out that Tim was taking on an identity toward *reading* as he prepared to *write*. Tim studied how others wrote constructive feedback, which taught him a way of approaching the fiction: "I want to know what's important so I read critiques, even if I haven't read the actual story, and that's a way of seeing what they like, what's good." He also studied how they wrote fiction. Tim described two interesting instances of using these examples as models. The first involved one sentence: "What really got me going was this very cool sentence by Elric [a forum writer]. It was this great action scene in one long sentence that made me move as a reader. I don't know how to do action scenes, so I pasted that sentence and rewrote it to fit my story. It ended up being a bit shorter, with different characters and weapons and stuff like that. By the end, I felt like it was mine. My writing. My ideas."

Tim could not find the original story on the forum, so I was unable to compare the sentences; however, he basically described "patchwriting," a strategy that moves writers from plagiarism to summary and paraphrase. As Rebecca Howard (1999) argues, patchwriting can be a "move toward membership in a discourse community, a means of learning unfamiliar language and ideas" (7). In this instance, Tim was learning how to write fiction in a way this community seemed to appreciate. When I asked Tim if he had a "larger sense of the fiction that the community likes," he misunderstood the question, but described how he "figured out how a good story should have a shape to it: so much on characters and to balance action and things like that." He joked "[reading] Tolkien ruined balance for me," but from reading other stories on this forum he gained a "sense of how a story should flow." Tim used models to figure out how to write for this community. Also interesting in these two examples is how, in composition terms, Tim seemed to examine stories at the local level, focusing on one sentence's construction, and the global level, attending to a story's organization.

Tim read from a writer's position, which taught him ways of reading and writing in this particular genre and forum. In this example, reading and writing are not contentious, but mutually reinforcing; the web enabled people of similar interests to create an "affinity space," where they could gather to share information and help each other pursue individual goals in a collective space (Gee 2004). I also note an interesting turn on Brandt's assertion that the "moral legacy" of reading is being undermined by a shift in the reading-writing relationship. Although it may not be a part of reading's moral heritage, Tim's appreciation for how he could get "lost" in the quality of the forum writers' words seems old-fashioned. He was not reading only to write, not merely imitating to take for his own. He was reading to savor language and imagination.

In the next example, Amy does not read-write with a particular community; rather, she draws from the wealth of rhetorical and literate resources available on the web to create a blog and a remix.

AMY'S RUNNING REMIX

Amy reported few problems in her transition to college. Like David and Tim, she stayed close to home, but she attended a private university. She liked how the university was small and attracted quality students—with enrollment under 3,000 students and over half ranked in the top 25 percent of their high school class—and the variety of sports for female students also appealed to her. As we talked in a busy coffee shop a few miles from her campus, she explained how adapting to different reading and writing situations was not that difficult. Amy gave some credit for this easy transition to a cohort of students she worked with in and out of class: "A lot of my teammates and I take the same classes, and we're dedicated to helping each other as [an athletic] team and as students. When we don't understand something [in class], we help each other. We read each other's papers, prep for tests together, and discuss the homework." Unlike Diana, Amy enrolled in a first-year composition course: "It's helped me adjust to college-level writing, and we go over a lot of different styles in class—fiction, essays, online information." She could not describe how she read and wrote differently in various classes beyond this statement: "That's how school is. You've got to do different things in science and in history." As I asked for more specific details about these different expectations, it became clear that Amy had some awareness of disciplinary conventions, but did not have a language for those conventions: "I don't know. There are different things you do for different classes. You have to think a little different to do the work they expect."

As Amy managed the transition to college writing, she also began to broaden her use of reading and writing on the web. In high school, Amy was not particularly interested in online activities. In college, however, she started reading blogs and became interested in starting her own: "Sometimes you can share too much on Facebook, and sometimes you want to share things with a smaller group. I'm looking at different blogging sites to see my options and to see how others do it." Reading from a writer's position, Amy read blogs to study how others constructed theirs. When I asked what she learned from reading others' blogs, Amy replied that she paid attention to "how the screen options are set up—colors and titles and menus on the side—and how people controlled how much visitors could know about them." At this stage, she was aware of how design issues affected her aesthetically, and she assumed what pleased her would be appealing to her audience. She also "looked for ideas, things I might write about. I've been reading random blogs, seeing what I like, seeing what interests me, how others respond in the comments and how the bloggers write back." She elaborated on this last point: "I've been impressed by how some bloggers responded to snippy, snarky people. I learned so much by how they shut down others politely—sometimes sarcastically—but without yelling and name-calling." I asked her why that was important to her; she responded: "Well, I'm sure I will run into snippy and snarky people online. I'm sure people will eventually say mean things—if I get any visitors at all. I want to know how others do that." Amy was already thinking about a potential audience and wanted to learn from other writers who were interacting with audiences. Amy was developing a sense of the blog as a genre, and she was drawing on blogs as rhetorical resources, most notably in terms of invention and arrangement. She also saw options for crafting a particular ethos, at least in respect to responding to audience comments.

Of vital importance to Amy was how a blog could narrow her audience to "a more select group," noting that "Facebook has become way too open to too many people I know." When I pointed out that blogs could invite an even wider audience, she gave this thoughtful response: "But who would want to read my blog? And I won't put things on there that I'll regret if strangers see them. I'll tell a few friends about it, but it won't have everyone I know on it. I'm not going to use my full name, so I doubt others will stalk me and find it." Amy recognized how Facebook and blogs provided different options for engaging with audiences. She thought about these sites in terms of delivery, and how they allowed her to limit or expand the distribution and circulation of information (Porter 2009). Particularly impressive was how she described the influence of genre and audience on Facebook's delivery choices: not only was the audience growing too big— "and it's almost impossible to cut out people without offending them"—but the expected pace of Facebook reading and writing seemed to encourage "bite-sized blogging." Her blog, on the other hand, could be "as long or as short as I want it to be. This morning, I wrote on my Facebook that 'I'm always almost out of toothpaste.' That's fine, [but] if I want to do something more I'll use this blog." After I inquired about what made the Facebook status "fine," she said, "It's not a big deal. It's kind of amusing. A small piece of life. That's what you do on Facebook."

Apparently, Amy was not aware of Facebook's limitations on her writing choices until she examined how blogs worked. I asked when she started to become aware of the differences, and she responded: "I love Facebook, but I'm getting bored with it. I [started to] read blogs and thought that this was something else I could do. I saw different options." As work in genre theory (Devitt 2004), schema theory (McCormick 1994), and rhetorical theory (Brent 1992) has illustrated, we make sense of a genre or of a particular reading when we place it in comparison to other genres and readings, by recognizing what something is and what it is not. This comparison occurs unconsciously much of the time, but Amy engaged in that comparison at a metacognitive level as she examined an alternative to Facebook. This kind of comparison is promoted on the web, with its fast and simple access to these genres that can be placed within close proximity to each other—users can flip between multiple texts through tabbed browsing with minimal delay.

When I asked about the content she might put on the blog, Amy said she had not decided yet: "I won't know until I start." However, she did describe a "ridiculous project" she had been working on that sounded like a series of remixed images; Amy did not use the words *remix* or *meme*, but she had encountered the phenomena they represented. Amy's "ridiculous project" began with this inspiration: "Do you remember that picture of the cheerleader who cheered for the wrong team? I always got a kick out of that, and I think when other people put her in other pictures—that was part of the inspiration." The other part of the inspiration was to mock herself, to "not take myself so seriously as an athlete because I can get really competitive. And then I remembered [that meme]."

After a picture circulated online that seemed to show a University of Southern California cheerleader celebrating a game-winning touchdown by the opposing team at the Rose Bowl, it did not take long for the cheerleader's image to be extracted from the original picture and inserted into other images. It became a meme, a concept that spreads among people and gets changed along the way. The cheerleader, with pom poms raised in victory, was soon depicted celebrating the wrong side of historical events: she stood next to the tanks rolling toward a lone protester in Tiananmen Square in 1989; she was present at JFK's funeral, juxtaposed with Kennedy Jr.'s solemn salute; she cheered the Hindenburg explosion, shown in black and white; and she appeared in many others, including Pablo Picasso's *Guernica*, with her image distorted to match the style of the painting. Amy described the meme as "wrong, but amusing."

In the remixes Amy created, she preferred to make herself the object of humor. The image at the core of the remixes was a picture of her running and stumbling: "It was taken in a parking lot. My friends and I were playing around, I was running and stumbled—it looks like I'm going to sneeze with the look on my face. And it's just a funny picture." Using Photoshop, she cut herself out of the picture and inserted that portion into other images, some historical, some popular, some personal. In these images, Amy can be seen at the edge of John Trumbull's painting *Declaration of Independence*, running away from the signers; on the moon, stumbling away from an Apollo astronaut; on the edge of a gun fight scene from *The Matrix*, with only one foot showing as she exits the scene; and in a few pictures with family and friends, Amy always running away. The editing of her own image was rough, as was its insertion into other images, which Amy readily admitted. Although Amy intended limited distribution of the images and did not see herself participating in a popular web phenomenon, she was using the USC cheerleader meme as a model, which was already modeled on other memes. An early version of the USC Cheerleader meme was the "Tourist Guy": a hoax photograph circulated after 9/11 that depicted a tourist standing on top of one of the twin towers as a plane headed toward the tower; after it was debunked, the "Tourist Guy" spread to other historical disaster images. A more recent version of the meme involves actor Leonardo DiCaprio, who was photographed happily strutting on the set of the film *Inception*; the odd moment of levity for the serious actor led others to crop the "strutting" image and insert it into various historical images. Many of these memes involve juxtaposing a single figure against an unexpected background. Such memes provide models for the creation of more remixes.

Amy had started work on a PowerPoint slideshow of the compiled images, but had not set them to music yet: "I think I'll use something by Kelly Clarkson or that old song 'Dust in the Wind.' Something ultra-serious and cheesy." When I asked what the purpose was behind the slideshow, she initially responded it was "just fun," but then as she talked more about the slideshow she revealed other purposes: "After graduation, some friends made videos of pictures of us hanging out together, and they would use music like 'Time of Your Life.' It was sweet. I just don't do 'sweet' without laughing. And so many TV shows do it—the serious scenes at the end of the episode with ultra-serious music that they're using to fill time and to sell music. It's easy drama. It annoys me." Amy intended to parody television drama montages and videos made by her friends. Although I never saw the finished version of the slideshow, I viewed Amy's clever opening: a black screen slowly faded in the title "Dust in the Wind." A few peaceful images of sunsets and blue skies appeared, then an image of Amy and her friends—then, abruptly, a remixed image of Amy running and stumbling away from the signers of the Declaration of Independence. In this rough cut, I could see a nascent parody.[3]

With this slideshow, Amy was not imitating a model in the same way Tim was in the fiction forum. She used irony and juxtaposition in a critical fashion, distancing herself from the imitation. The work involved is not simple: "Appropriation may be understood as a process that involves both analysis and commentary. Sampling intelligently from the existing cultural reservoir requires a close analysis of the existing structures and uses of this material; remixing requires an appreciation of emerging structures and latent potential meanings" (Jenkins et al. 2006, 33). Amy had already developed a critical perspective regarding television shows that used montages to "fill time and sell music." To effectively mock the videos made by friends, she had to study—or at least be aware of—their structure. Through creating her own remixes, she analyzed and perceived structures of existing remixes and memes. The rough cut of the video did not last long, but the extensive thinking Amy put into it was clear from how she could articulate the remix with me.

Appropriating the work of others is not new. Sampling and remixing are novel practices only in how widespread they have become, due to the ease of finding materials online and technologies that allow novices to manipulate those materials. Some websites have even simplified the process for contributing to a meme, providing a "meme generator" that allows users to select an image, enter text, and then the site generates the result. Advanced editing programs for video and sound can be downloaded for free, and program users can help each other by sharing advice through online tutorials and message boards. Such technologies have helped spur sampling by musicians, both novice and professional: Girl Talk's album *Night Ripper* remixed over 200 samples from 167 artists (Lessig 2008, 11); in 2009, Kutiman released a music album through YouTube made entirely of YouTube clips of individual, mostly amateur musicians who had never met, which he then remixed into coherent songs (Thill 2009). The web is a repository of materials, practices, and affinity spaces that encourage various forms of literacy.

READING-WRITING BOUNDARIES

From Lauren's image-filled business proposal that began this chapter, to Tim's and Amy's attempts to engage online forms of writing, this chapter has examined how the web provides rhetorical and literate resources for readers and writers. This examination provides an alternative perspective on the reading-writing relationship; more people are reading from the perspective of a writer, but this seems to be a relationship that mutually reinforces both forms of literate activity. Indeed, if more people are reading from the perspective of a writer more often, is it not likely they are also writing from the position of a potential reader, as well? My discussion with Amy about how she read blogs and intended to write her own signaled a strong awareness of genre and audience; she was thinking about what worked in a particular genre and what might work for a particular audience. This suggests a fluid, cooperative relationship between reading and writing. As literacy accumulates online, people find more material to work with as readers and writers, as well as many places that offer collaboration and modeling, just as Tim did. Tim's example speaks to the importance of the social context in which imitation occurs. When specific affinity spaces do not exist, the spreading out of literate materials can be drawn upon as resources, which was how Amy became interested in blogs and remixes. These examples illustrate the power of imitation, of models that readers draw from as they pursue their own writing. They demonstrate the benefits of accumulation and acceleration, of having literacy options and the fast, convenient access to those options.

Of course, seeing Amy and Tim use models to approach reading and writing with such confidence outside of school raises a question: Did they seek out and use models—or at least their reading-writing strategies for imitation—in college? A similar question could be asked of the reading strategies I observed from David and Diana in chapter four: Did they use such strategies in college reading? When I asked the participants questions about bringing such strategies into their academic reading and writing, they reacted with confusion. Amy, Tim, and David gave largely empty, pause-filled responses to the suggestion that the kind of modeling they used on the web could also function in school. Amy's question of "How would I even do that?" and Tim's statement that the "stuff you do online is just different" gave the impression that they regarded in-school and out-of-school practices as separate, not to be crossed. Diana offered that she "probably use[s] some of the skimming" strategies in college reading, but the similarities ended there: "School research is so different, and I think about how it needs to be done for school." Lauren and her friends from the beginning of the chapter are an interesting anomaly; they consciously brought out-of-school practices into their written proposals. I wonder if they felt so comfortable "bending the rules" because they were "experts" at high school writing and were so close to graduation.

Of course, the issue of transfer is complex. It is possible students may transfer a strategy or skill without being aware of it or being able to articulate such transference (Wardle 2007). But beliefs about literacy matter; they shape what people do with literacy. Amy, Tim, Diana, and David expressed confusion at the thought of merging in-school and out-of-school practices; they did not seem to think it should even happen. In their study of genre transference, Mary Jo Reiff and Anis Bawarshi (2011) found that first-year composition (FYC) students reported a "wealth of genre knowledge in school, work, and other domains," yet they "tended not to report drawing on the full range of their genre knowledge when they encountered and performed new writing tasks in FYC" (323). An academic essay prompt reminded the students of other school-based genres, not genres from other life domains (324). For Reiff and Bawarshi, this result "suggests that students might assume such a strong correspondence between particular genres and specific domains that they may not call on (or may not be aware that they are calling on) potentially useful resources that they associate with other domains" (324). Without specific guidance that directs students to draw from genres and strategies from other domains, students "may be too locked into domains to consider a full range of genre resources and strategies for responding" (331). Perhaps Diana and the other participants were still too "locked into domains" to consciously draw from their out-of-school literacy practices.

A systematic examination of transfer was beyond the scope of this study, but the question of how students regard domain boundaries—particularly those between school and home—is an important one. As composition continues to expand its sense of writing and incorporate genres students more readily identify with other, non-school domains, it is essential that the field pursues a more nuanced understanding of how students perceive domains and the literacy practices that accumulate within and between those domains. As the previous chapters have shown, the participants have thoughtful, engaging practices with literacy and rhetoric. Finding ways to help students draw on the literate, rhetorical resources they possess may bolster not only what they do with reading and writing in college but in other domains as well, allowing them to realize, appreciate, and capitalize on the potential of their everyday literacies.

NOTES

1   At the time of this writing, *The Daily Prophet* had gone offline due to Lawver's long-term illness.

2   For a fascinating and extensive examination of fan fiction before the web, see Jenkins' (1992) *Textual Poachers*.

3   In an e-mail, Amy informed me further work on her blog and remixes was postponed as her school work became more difficult.

CONCLUSION

What does it mean to be a reader in the twenty-first century? One goal of this book has been to gain more insight into the challenges and opportunities for literacy learners in a time of accumulation and acceleration. As literacies accumulate, readers encounter both an increasing number of texts and wide variation in how those texts are packaged in genres and delivered through media. When confronted with a staggering number of texts, readers must respond with filtering strategies and tools to direct their limited time and attention wisely. With the great variety of textual shapes, they also must learn to adapt reading strategies to different texts and contexts. Acceleration is one response to accumulation, to the overabundance of texts and media options: when faced with so many texts, readers tend to read faster, skimming, scanning, and sorting. Proficient readers throughout history have most likely responded to an abundance of texts with filtering strategies (Blair 2003). However, the demands of contemporary literacy mean that more people must develop more methods of oscillating between faster and slower forms of reading, and between hyper and deep ranges of attention. Moreover, acceleration is not exclusively a phenomenon of literacy: it is a confluence of cultural forces that reinforces the values of speed and efficiency. Although acceleration can be identified in many parts of contemporary life, the values associated with speed and efficiency are also embedded in contemporary literacy practices, particularly those involving communication technologies.

In chapter four, David's multimedia coffee table was an exemplar of accumulation, with layers of media options—a book, comic book, magazine, cell phone, TV controller, video game controller, etc.—within his reach. David's laptop and wireless connection provided access to a wide expanse of genres and media. His

DOI: 10.7330/9780874219333.c006

multitasking across literacy activities was a strategy adapted to the demands of acceleration, and Diana and Tim also multitasked to manage and compare information sources. Increasingly, more people will access and read texts on laptops, smartphones, and various electronic reading devices. Book-length texts will continue to be read on such devices; however, the mobile nature of the devices combined with other accelerating forces will encourage speed and brevity and increase the pressure to "keep up" as readers and writers. This pressure promotes particular "fast" literacy practices. For instance, in chapter three, participants described a kind of ephemeral rhetoric they engaged in through social network reading and writing. Contemporary readers may have to learn not only how to direct their own attention when filtering information, but how to gauge the speed of rhetoric in different situations in order to thoughtfully produce rhetorics that will gain and direct the attention of others.

Despite the unmistakable influence of communication technologies, the early twenty-first century reader does not rely exclusively on digital media. Participants in chapter three talked about combining print and digital formats to achieve particular goals, whether it was Nadia reading print history books and online news about Iraq, or Mark reading fiction in print and then reading online discussion forums to supplement his understanding. The participants' experiences demonstrate that one aspect of early twenty-first century reading and writing is the practice of shuttling between print and digital texts. This shuttling requires fluency with literacy practices of both formats and the capacity to make decisions about when to seek or produce ideas, stories, and information in one format or the other. Such decisions are often made in contexts in which multiple texts and media compete for attention, so participants had to make choices about the practices they would value and pursue. Readers will continue to shuttle between these forms of reading and make conscious decisions about what they can achieve through various media.

A significant change in contemporary reading and writing involves the speed and convenience with which one can shift from the role of reader to writer (Brandt 2009). Acceleration is a factor in this development, because faster processing speeds and the development of technologies that allow easy reading-writing shifts reflect the value our society places in staying connected and keeping up. Fast, fluid shifts between reader and writer roles are also facilitated by the material shapes of technologies—keyboards, copy-and-paste tools, and touch screens that serve as an interface for both reading and writing—and the social relationships that surround and infuse the practices of reading and writing. The social aspects of the web provide an ever-accumulating repository of materials, practices, and affinity spaces, a repository a large number of people can draw from and contribute to. Not only *can* something someone reads be responded to immediately, but the social nature of the web often *encourages* and *rewards* those responses. A benefit of this alternating, reciprocal relationship between reading and writing may be an increased sense of audience awareness. For instance, Amy's discussion of her blog demonstrated she was thinking about how a particular audience might react to specific elements of her blog; as she read the blogs of others, she paid attention to how those bloggers responded to their audiences. In other words, in the prewriting stages of her blog, Amy was writing from a reader's perspective, and as she examined other blogs, she read as a writer. Although good writers have always been concerned with audience needs and have sought models in the texts of others, the immediacy with which readers can become writers—and vice versa—on the web may make such a reading/writing strategy more habitual to those familiar with online literacy spaces.

As the above description illustrates, contemporary reading is shaped by techno-cultural contexts that are not accounted for by existing composition pedagogy. Although the field has pursued new ways of composing, we have let reading get away from us. We need to regard, study, and teach reading and writing as complementary acts of literacy. A new reading pedagogy would help students meet the challenges and capitalize on the opportunities presented in a time of fast literacy change. Pedagogy is not merely a collection of strategies and assignments; rather, it is a theorized, coherent vision of how learning happens and what will benefit students. It is informed by research. As a starting point to this research and pedagogy on reading, consider these four significant features of literacy learning that emerged in this study: accumulation and curricular choices, literacy perceptions, speeds of rhetoric, and speeds of reading.

ACCUMULATION AND CURRICULAR CHOICES

The concept of literacy accumulation has given scholars a framework for understanding how literacy changes and how contemporary literacy learners face steep challenges as they negotiate receding, merging, and emerging literacies (Brandt 1995). As they move among various domains, literacy users must position and reposition themselves amidst changing literacies. Throughout this book, I have applied the concept of accumulation to the concerns of composition pedagogy and research. In particular, accumulation can help us think about the choices we—as individual teachers, as writing program administrators, and as a field—must make about what to teach and, by extension, what the purpose and scope of composition—the class and the discipline—ought to be. That is, given the wide and ever-growing range of literacy practices, where should composition direct its energy and time? As a consequence of choosing to teach particular literacy practices, what other practices are marginalized or left out?

I traced two sets of literacy value choices evident in composition research and pedagogy in chapter one, where I recounted composition's marginalization of reading theory/pedagogy and the field's more recent expansion of what counts as writing to include multimodal forms of composition. Both the marginalization of reading and the expansion of writing practices have implications for the how the field defines itself, the resources teachers will need in order to keep up with this expansion, and what students learn about what it means to be literate at the college level. As literacies accumulate, composition must position and reposition itself amidst receding, merging, and emerging literacies, as well as in respect to its purposes and responsibilities.

Doug Hesse (2010) has articulated two questions for the field in light of this ongoing expansion of writing. The first question asks how we will define composition—as rhetoric (open to multiple composition forms) or as writing (open to fewer forms, mostly alphabetic text)? He urges the field to seek a resolution to this question with the "full participation of all stakeholders in composition courses, especially if they're required" (603). Hesse makes clear his commitment to being transparent with stakeholders about the definition and work of composition. Closely related to the first question is the second: "Whose interests should the composition class serve?" (603). To what extent is it our responsibility to prepare students for the rest of college, for the workforce, and for engaging in civic discourse? As we choose the literacy practices to teach, we must keep in mind the effects those curricular choices may have on our ability to fulfill our responsibilities to the range of stakeholders with a vested interest in what happens in the composition classroom.

Regarding Hesse's thoughtful argument, I think accumulation and acceleration can be useful concepts in the discussion about composition's curricular boundaries and purposes because they provide a framework for understanding the pressures shaping the curriculum. They illuminate the challenges of resolving the issue, particularly when it involves teachers and students—important stakeholders—who have unequal literacy resources. As I have argued, literacies don't simply accumulate neutrally; they are always attached to particular sets of values, values that may compete with those attached to another set of literacy practices. Some post-secondary institutions will value certain literacy practices over others, promoting some and not others. Literacies don't accumulate equally, either. Because literacy resources and contexts vary, teachers and students at one institution may have greater access to literacies than other institutions. That is, one particular school might value new literacies, have faculty with the pedagogical/theoretical tools to teach new literacies, and possess the institutional resources to support new literacies. Another institution might not have the same conditions.

Virginia Anderson (2010) voices her concerns about teachers' unequal access to technological resources in her thoughtful essay, "Supply-Side Dreams: Composition, Technology, and the Circular Logic of Class." The challenges posed by accumulation and acceleration can be heard throughout her essay as she argues, "contrary to a thread of the dominant discourse that contends that technological change is an unstoppable train, composition as a field need not be a breathless passenger as these material challenges accumulate" (125). Anderson is not against teaching with technology, nor is she arguing we should slow down as a field. However, she interrogates the assumption that "keeping up with and exploiting technological innovation will benefit literacy educators"; she acknowledges that at the core of this assumption is the well-intentioned goal of helping students become more capable and critical users of technology. Yet, Anderson argues a "too-exuberant embrace of this assumption can blind" us to teachers' unequal access to technology resources, as well as the uneven costs paid by teachers (125). The scholarship raising the bar on new media pedagogy often comes from those with the resources—the time, the technology, the support—to experiment and learn; when others with fewer resources try to reach that bar, the results can be frustrating and even counterproductive to effective pedagogy. As literacy accumulates, as our teaching options expand, we have to make decisions about when and how to spend our energy and time. Pursuing the latest technology or new media practice may not be the most pedagogically sound decision given a teacher's available resources. Anderson points out "when there is still so much to be learned about how much any particular innovation actually increases learning, there is somewhat more urgency in critically examining the differential in time devoted to learning software versus time devoted to other forms of teaching" (135). Furthermore, Anderson observes that the "Digital Divide" intensifies class divisions among teachers; those who pursue critical technology practices are regarded as responsible educators, and those who do not, by comparison and default, then become marked as irresponsible for not keeping up (136). To put Anderson's argument in terms of accumulation, the literacy practices associated with "new" and "digital" signal a value of responsible pedagogy, and those literacies primarily associated with "traditional" may be devalued. As literacies accumulate and accelerate, the divisions between these teachers may grow even wider.

I do not point out these complications to deem Hesse's (2010) questions unresolvable. Rather, I see them as important contours that should shape the discussion of the field's identity, its curricular boundaries, and its responsibilities. The concepts of accumulation and acceleration can provide us with a stance, a sense of distance from which we can see the changing terrain of literacy. Instead of being caught up in the movement of literacy, this distance can help us make more conscious choices about literacy. Acceleration, for instance, calls attention to new practices and leads to questions about how those new practices will fit into an existing curriculum. It should also make us more aware of curricular "clutter—the piling on of objectives and requirements—that makes any form of sustained work difficult" (Newkirk 2009, 11). Although I promote faster rhetorics and faster forms of reading, I would not want them to contribute to shallow, brief literacy activities in the classroom. Even though I want more attention to reading in the classroom, this does not mean more readings need to be assigned; indeed, students may learn more from fewer readings that students reread with different strategies and purposes. I value a slow curriculum that makes room for repeated, reinforced experiences that support connection, practice, and metacognition.

Composition should continue to expand its study and teaching of new forms of reading and writing. Composition teachers, however, might be wise to think more strategically about literacy practices, rather than about specific media. Instead of multiple, shallow encounters with many media, students might benefit more from a sustained focus on a few media, with an emphasis on how and why readers and writers choose and use particular communication channels. Without that focus, the result can be a cluttered curriculum, in which teachers end up, at best, chasing literacy, pursuing the next development and never feeling grounded; at worst, the temptation to fill one course with every significant form of digital and traditional composing would result in a shallow form of "digital literacies tourism."

LITERACY PERCEPTIONS

The concept of life domains—the "structured, patterned contexts within which literacy is used and learned"—has helped scholars study how literacy operates at various sites of literate activity (Barton and Hamilton 1998, 10). The structures and patterns of literacies within domains are influenced by the social institutions connected to those domains; for instance, family and education are social institutions connected to home and school, and those institutions have informal and formal ways of regulating and shaping what occurs with literacy. Schools (and homes) do not always regulate and shape literacy in the same way, which is why scholars focus on local, situated accounts of literacy. However, social institutions tend to produce similar patterns, with education's support of formalized, dominant literacies over "vernacular" literacies being an example (10–11). Domains do not have solid boundaries, but have "leakages and movement between boundaries" and "overlap between domains" (10). Composition teachers need a better understanding of that movement and overlap as they attempt to bring more literacies commonly associated with other domains into the composition classroom. For example, an overlooked part of how students adapt literacy practices to different contexts is how their perceptions of literacy are influenced by cultural narratives. In chapter two, I elaborated on Brandt's concept of accumulation to explain some of the tension that exists when teachers and students try to bring literacies across domains. As literacies circulate through domains, they become marked with narratives that travel with them into other domains. The narratives literacies pick up as they cross domains ultimately influence how those literacies will be perceived, regulated, and used in particular domains. Cultural narratives about specific literacies not only accumulate in layers at the original sites in which those literacies were practiced, but also travel with literacies as they circulate across domains.

Perceptions affect what people do with literacy. As the participant interviews suggested, perceptions of reading in school influenced the reading strategies participants used in school; in particular, the participants understood in- and out-of-school reading to be separate acts and so did not apply out-of-school literacy strategies to classroom assignments, even when such strategies might have been helpful. Mary Jo Reiff and Anis Bawarshi (2011) found similar results in their study of students who had a wide range of genre knowledge from different domains. Despite the breadth of the students' knowledge, they had difficulty applying that knowledge across domain boundaries. Reiff and Bawarshi suspected this difficulty may have resulted from the students' being "too locked into domains to consider a full range of genre resources and strategies" (331). That is, when faced with school assignments, the students drew from genres associated with school, not other domains. The question of how to help students draw upon literacy resources within a particular domain and across different domains is vital, especially considering the complex connections students are expected to make among media they compose and read in composition classrooms. For instance, in Kathleen Yancey's (2004) suggested curriculum, students are asked to "think explicitly about what they might 'transfer' from one medium to the next: what moves forward, what gets left out, what gets added—and what they have learned about composing in this transfer process"; they are also asked to think about how "what they have learned" might transfer to another site of literacy (311). Yancey's encouragement of metacognitive reflection on media and domain transference is an excellent suggestion for making such work more focused on critical literacy practices than on technology application. Students' reflective writing about their multimodal compositions has become fairly common; not only is it a thoughtful method for promoting metacognition with literacy practices, but it is also a way to produce more writing in the composition classroom. However, composition still has a lot to learn about how we might help students engage in sophisticated reflection on how literacy circulates and changes.

More research is needed on students' perceptions and uses of literacies in various domains and their sense of the crossover among social institutions. One significant area of such research is on the transition between high school and college. As Reiff and Bawarshi point out, most of composition's research "has focused on what skills, habits, strategies, and knowledge learned in FYC courses transfer to and enable students to succeed in other disciplinary and workplace contexts." Composition has fewer studies on and less knowledge regarding "what transfers *into* FYC" (315, italics original). What transfers into FYC is shaped by how students perceive literacy and how literacy experiences can be connected. How do students perceive the literacy expectations of high school and college? What sociocultural influences shape those perceptions? How do those perceptions affect their literate performances? What connections do they make between in-school and out-of-school literacies? If they have difficulty making such connections, what might be the obstacles?

SLOWER/FASTER RHETORICS

I have argued that acceleration is a defining feature of contemporary literacy. When multiple cultural forces promote speed and efficiency, communication technologies will increasingly accelerate along with those forces, promoting rhetorical and literacy practices that value speed. Acceleration acts as a rhetorical force, influencing the delivery choices of rhetors in digital contexts. While interpreting participant interviews, I connected their choices of short, fast messages to James Porter's (2009) theory of digital delivery, of which *distribution* and *circulation* are key components; distribution involves decisions about how to package a message, and circulation involves the potential for that message to spread and get repackaged (214). The participants engaged in ephemeral distribution, brief rhetorics aimed at gaining attention; they were less concerned with circulation. Circulation—how texts spread and change—is the feature of rhetoric that has traditionally interested composition, and I worry that we may undervalue distribution, especially the fading rhetoric practiced by these participants. I also think ephemeral distribution is a significant, common aspect of digital communication. Certainly, bloggers and Twitter users want their messages linked and retweeted, but a more common goal may be to maintain recurring attention. As Colin Lankshear and Michele Knobel (2003) argue, attention is an important commodity when information is abundant, and "people's efforts to attract, sustain, and build attention under new media conditions" will continue to be a crucial part of literacy practices (109–10).

Because fleeting rhetoric often involves trivial matters—the quality of coffee, the contents of lunch—it can be dismissed easily. However, we may be overlooking the "social glue" such rhetoric provides in online environments, just as people in face-to-face encounters exchange trivial pleasantries about the weather. In my interviews and observations, I asked participants how they intended their messages to be read and how they learned the discourse rules for such messages, but the way readers interpret and respond to ephemeral rhetorics is also a potential research area. How does ephemeral rhetoric contribute to the "social glue" of online communication? Does it perform other social or discursive functions?

Ephemeral rhetorics have other implications as well. The participants' literacy practices demonstrated that Lester Faigley's (2006) binary of "fast/slow rhetorics" might productively be refigured as a continuum of faster and slower rhetorics. In contrast to Faigley's recommendation that we focus on teaching slow rhetoric for the good of civic discourse, I argue we should study and teach a range of rhetorical speeds. Faigley's statement that we know "what slow rhetoric can accomplish" (7) raises an important, unanswered question: What can faster rhetorics accomplish? To briefly pursue this question, I want to turn to the Hesse-Selfe discussion regarding the boundaries and responsibilities of composition. As Hesse (2010) ponders FYC's responsibility to civic debate, he points to examples of shallow rhetoric occurring in the national debate over health care legislation: "As I'm writing, national health care reform is generating huge volumes of rhetorical activity; I long for more reasoned and developed rationales than the glib sound and image bites proffered from all angles" (605). In her response, Cynthia Selfe (2010) takes issue with how Hesse "equates 'more reasoned and developed rationales' with the *written word*, and less reasoned 'glib' reasoning with 'sound[s] and image[s]'" (608, italics original). Selfe observes that "glib" discussions about health care reform also appeared in print essays; furthermore, she argues she found some multimodal texts on the issue to be "well reasoned, well documented, carefully thought out, and informative." Ultimately, she concludes, "no one medium or modality—certainly not writing—has a corner on reason, thoughtfulness, effectiveness, *or* glibness" (609, italics original). I agree with Selfe in regard to modal determinism; however, I want to redirect their discussion by wondering how faster rhetorics, even those not be particularly "well documented" or especially "informative," might remain thoughtful and responsible elements of civic discourse.

In the health care reform debate mentioned by Hesse and Selfe, a good example of irresponsible rhetoric would be the "death panel" myth. In "Why the 'Death Panel' Myth Wouldn't Die," political scientist Brendan Nyhan (2010) tracks the origin and spread of the "death panel" myth, the claim by pundits and politicians that "health care legislation in Congress would result in seniors being directed to 'end their life [sic] sooner'" (8). The myth inflamed public discourse, especially at town hall meetings where concerned citizens voiced their opposition to such a plan. Although it is difficult to state the ultimate effect of this myth on public opinion, Nyhan points out "if even a fraction of the people who believed these myths turned against reform as a result, the aggregate effect on public opinion was likely to have been highly significant" (4–5). Nyhan traces the spread of the myth through various media, noting the "speed with which the myth took hold is especially striking" compared to the speed at which health care myths spread in the early 1990s (11). The accelerated spreading of the "death panel" myth points to the value of studying and teaching a range of rhetorical speeds. In a time when messages can spread and shape opinions so quickly, is it realistic and responsible to urge only slower rhetorics? How might a response to "death panels" have been constructed as fast, thoughtful, and informative? It is not hard to imagine that a fast rhetoric could have been deployed not only to challenge the "death panel" myth, but also to direct attention to slower rhetorics providing more information. How can faster rhetorics be harnessed in effective and ethical ways? Given composition's commitment to civic discourse, what opportunities do we lose by leaving faster rhetorics unexamined?

A renewed reading theory could help inform rhetorical theory/practice across the continuum, from fast to slow. Doug Brent's (1992) *Reading as Rhetorical Invention* is the last book-length attempt in composition scholarship to pursue a model of how readers construct the rhetorical efforts of writers. Continued theoretical work combined with empirical studies of reader responses to various persuasive efforts may offer a richer sense of how rhetoric achieves or fails to achieve particular effects. This work on how readers construct the rhetoric of others could inform our efforts to study and teach a range of rhetorical speeds. It could also assist our understanding of how students read the persuasive efforts of classroom texts. Currently, composition teachers have rhetorical concepts and argumentation models that are supposed to guide students' rhetorical reading, but these resources deserve augmentation with knowledge of how students perceive and perform rhetorical reading. Without that augmentation, without connecting the educational model of rhetorical reading to the models of reading students bring into the classroom, I wonder about the effectiveness of such pedagogy.

On a final pedagogical note, I would offer slower-faster rhetorics as vocabulary for classroom teaching. If the participants in the study and the students in my classrooms are any indication, students grasp the concept of speed in very real ways. The concepts of slower and faster rhetorics can enrich discussions of delivery choices, of how genres and media might give texts not only different shapes but different speeds, and how rhetorical choices affect which audience a text will reach and how much attention audience members will devote to it. Such discussions can also provide an opportunity to talk about why slower rhetorics are employed so often in academic reading and writing, which can lead students to approach that work in more informed ways.

SPEEDS OF READING

Multitasking deserves closer examination for three reasons: first, multimodal composition tends to use technologies that demand a high level of multitasking; second, online reading can be considered a form of multitasking because of the many options readers have for directing and re-directing their attention; third, the popular narrative constructed about multitasking tends to conflate different tasks and purposes into a generalized claim that multitasking is ineffective. After observing David, Diana, and Tim multitask so skillfully, I developed two concepts for the kinds of reading I witnessed. The first I called *foraging*, a purposeful wandering across texts, evaluating and possibly gathering and using materials along the way. For instance, Diana's comparisons of news stories involved gathering keywords from search results and using them in future searches. The second kind of reading strategy I witnessed involved *oscillating* between levels of depth and rates of speed. Diana and Tim each oscillated between different levels of depth: reading at shallow levels as they quickly skimmed and scanned the screen; and reading deeply, not necessarily the whole text, perhaps a fragment, which they sometimes read a few times. They also oscillated between rates of speed: reading quickly, then slowly; fast reading was sometimes followed by a focusing stop. Speeds of reading are shaped by the kinds of attention readers want and need to give to a text.

I would not want to argue that all multitasking is effective, or even as wisely enacted as it was in these observed instances with the participants. In fact, I would argue that a distinction could be made between intentional and unintentional multitasking. Intentional multitasking is performed with awareness of one's purpose in multitasking, the limitations of one's own attention, and strategies for multitasking effectively and decreasing unwanted distractions. Unintentional multitasking is when people engage in multitasking thoughtlessly, or have multitasking thrust upon them. It occurs almost haphazardly, with little awareness of the limits of one's attention, little conscious decision-making about how he or she will multitask, and a high likelihood of unproductive distraction. It is often accidental, prone to admit new tasks and purposes that pull away from the reader's original purposes. The difference between intentional and unintentional multitasking is exemplified in David's conscious decision to play a simple online video game between alternating to other activities, a choice made with awareness of the demands of the tasks he shifted among; a less controlled form of multitasking might have resulted in a more difficult game choice, or the choice of additional tasks and texts that were less familiar to David. The range of multitasking behavior between *intentional* and *unintentional* offers a much more useful way to understand multitasking than the popular narrative, which tends to obscure what can be a complex literacy act. In order to ascertain a more nuanced understanding of David's multitasking, I devised the following heuristic:

- Task: specific activity, includes purpose and context
- Tactic: reading strategy
- Text: message, includes the genre and medium
- Technology: device and interface used to access the text, includes search engines and other on-screen interfaces
- Training: experience and knowledge of the other four factors

These five characteristics of multitasking are essential to our concerns as teachers of reading and writing, especially the reading tactic/strategy, which is often not controlled for in studies of multitasking/hypertext reading (Salmeron et al. 2005).

The heuristic and the more nuanced picture of multitasking I have offered can point to future research in this area. Many of the studies performed on multitasking involve controlled settings or a test of knowledge, but these are not as relevant to composition as the authentic settings and everyday goals of students' literacy practices. How do students multitask as they pursue their own interests outside of school? How do they use multitasking when researching for school? Researchers could record and observe these activities according to a method/ scheme similar to the exploratory version described in this book. Researchers could also create more controlled studies and minimize the effects of their presence by using screen-capture software to record specific research tasks performed by multiple students. What research methods did the students use? How did they use multitasking efficiently or inefficiently, intentionally or unintentionally? Such studies could be undertaken with a range of students, from undergraduate to graduate, from novice to expert.

Additional research could pursue methods associated with cognitive psychology. Chris Anson and Robert Schwegler (2012) recommend the use of eye-tracking technology to study the relationship between reading and writing, which would revive composition's work with cognitive research and offer "ways to understand previously inaccessible dimensions of writing and reading that extend well beyond psychologically based studies of discourse processes" (152). Anson and Schwegler indicate several areas of research that could be studied with the technology, including the "relationship of visual and textual information in both composing and reading onscreen" (152). As I noted in chapter one, composition's backlash against the perceived scientism of cognitive studies led to diminished research in that area. As Anson and Schwegler argue, the research they recommend "does not ignore the social, cultural, and contextual dimensions of writing but supplements and enhances them" (163). These studies can help scholars and teachers learn more about how students direct their attention through reading, which can lead to pedagogical approaches that promote conscious choices and metacognition.

CHASING LITERACY

Effective twenty-first century readers engage in highly complex literacy practices. For these readers, literacy is almost always in motion (sometimes literally, as reading devices allow mobile access to a range of reading materials). They may feel as if they are always chasing something: the latest upgrade, the latest tweet or Facebook post (including reactions to their own posts), the "good" source amid millions of Google hits, and strategies for managing multitasked reading and writing. These readers look much like twenty-first century writers, who are also chasing new composing technologies, audiences and affinity spaces, good sources of information, and genre models for their own creations. And, of course, by participating in the literacy chase, readers and writers propel it along, contributing to the pressure to keep up. Literacy users are complicit as they participate in the cycle of responding to and further advancing accumulation and acceleration. Although literacy is constantly accumulating and accelerating, demanding more and more from literacy learners and teachers, we are not powerless in the face of such demands. Our participation means we can give some shape to the conditions of literacy. Because the composition classroom engages the complex, situated aspects of rhetoric and literacy, we have a unique position to pause amid the chase with students to survey our literacy practices and choose how we participate. The literacy chase need not be a relentless race. Instead, it can be a conscientious pursuit of reading and writing practices that allow people some measure of control over how literacy influences them and how they influence literacy.

APPENDIX

This study was approved by the Institutional Review Board.
All participant names are pseudonyms.

MIDWEST HIGH SCHOOL

The nine student participants attended Midwest High School, a school with a population of nearly 1,700 students located in an urban area. It is an excellent school, but its excellence is also complicated. Over 90 percent of its graduates go on to post-secondary education. On state and national tests, it meets and exceeds standards. *US News and World Report* gives it a high rating in the state for reading and writing; however, this rating is based on the number of Advanced Placement courses offered by the school. As the school's English teachers discussed with me, the importance of such ratings can lead to an increase in Advanced Placement courses when students may not be prepared for them. Because of its reputation, Midwest is not easy to get into: the application overload is sorted by lottery. The school has diversity of race and gender, but not as much in economic status. The low number of students eligible for food stamps has prevented funding for remedial training and courses; as a result, some students flounder when compared to the better-prepared students. The teacher Julia commented on this problem: "Some students struggle a lot, and teachers struggle with how to help those students. The funding isn't there."

During my visits to the school, I was struck by the energy in the hallways and in the classrooms. As the teachers concurred, Midwest has motivated, energetic students who genuinely appreciate their school. Such qualities make teaching a little bit easier, but much of the teaching for such an excellent school is based

DOI: 10.7330/9780874219333.c007

around tests and the top-down model of learning. The school's above-average standing was one of my reasons for choosing it as a site of study: How do "good readers" read in and out of school?

PARTICIPANTS

Julia has over twenty years of teaching experience and is a senior teacher at Midwest. Energetic and enthusiastic about her students and her school, she is also critical and aware of the many limitations regarding how her students learn.

Angela is the director of the library. She created a social space in the library with living room furniture, and included popular fiction and graphic novels in the library's collection.

Mark is an above-average student and a voracious reader, consuming literary classics as well as popular fiction. One of his earliest statements involved his love of challenging literature: "I enjoy reading things I don't understand very well, things I have to work at. I often try to read above what is expected of me."

James is also an above-average student and a voracious reader. Quiet and unassuming, he and the more outgoing Mark are friends and the only participants to know of each other's involvement in the study. James often spoke of the pleasure he gets from reading: "I love reading, and I have a hard time understanding people who don't like it. Even if you don't like it, you should do it. Life seems pretty hard if you're not good at reading and don't try at it. I do well at school, and I learn a lot and feel so much more from the reading I do for myself."

Nadia is the only EFL (English as a Foreign Language) student in the study, having moved to the United States from Iraq when she was four. Bright and confident, Nadia sees her foreign-language background as a reason for her academic success: it makes her think harder about language compared to students who've only had "one language rolling around their heads for most of their lives." She was described by other participants as one of the few students who would argue—skillfully, no less—with English teachers about her interpretations. Nadia is the only non-white participant in the study.

Sarah is heavily involved in sports, but also manages to excel in academics. She is motivated to do well in school because it has been expected of her: "I can't say that I love school or that I deeply love learning. Most of the time, I do my work because I should."

Lauren is also good at sports and academics. She describes herself as a good reader, but claims not to read often. As Amy and David would also reveal, they read more than expected once I expanded the definition of reading beyond literature.

Amy is a self-described average reader. She and David both talk about the importance of vocabulary and keywords. However, despite her lack of confidence in her reading, Amy does very well in most of her courses. Amy and the remaining students stayed in the study after the high school portion was completed. Amy did well in her transition to college.

David does not like reading. He reads more than he suspects, but he struggles with school reading. The visit to David's home, and the vast array of media surrounding David, inspired the topics of attention and multitasking.

Tim loves reading, but he has personal and political differences when it comes to the way his teachers discuss literature. He seems full of potential, but does average work. He and David struggled in the transition to college.

Diana is the overachiever. She earns college credit for some of her high school courses. She's motivated and smart, but she also knows how to look motivated and smart while cutting corners. Although she found some elements of the college transition frustrating, she generally did well in her classes.

METHODS

Even though I wanted to study "good" readers at an above-average high school, I also wanted a wide range of readers within that setting; that is, I hoped to recruit students who regarded themselves as "bad" readers as well. The recruitment stage of the study may explain the small number of participants. I pitched the study to multiple English classes at Midwest. Most of the classes did not ask any questions about the study, but in one particularly outspoken group, a few students responded to the phrase "a study about reading" with statements such as "You wouldn't want me. I don't like reading." I assured them I wanted a range of students, but the perception might have been too much to overcome. Other students might have been turned away at the thought of being tested on reading; although I gave no indication of an exam, two participants asked me when I would give them a reading test.

The study was exploratory. The interviews were designed with general questions about reading, which would then lead to more open-ended discussions based on the participants' responses. I interviewed the participants multiple times and gathered literacy histories (Barton and Hamilton, 1998). I wanted to see how their responses might change over time, which involved asking similar questions about reading and writing at different times. I audio-recorded the interviews and took field notes during and after interviews. I examined the transcripts and field notes for repeated phrases and themes, and these transcripts and notes informed my questions in the next set of interviews. For instance, I had not intended to examine curricular speed or the pressure of keeping up with technology; these themes became interesting because of how many times they appeared in the interviews. The exploratory nature also allowed me to adjust to unexpected limitations. I had intended to gather more data, including syllabi, assignments, and multiple class observations (at high school and college) as a larger part of the study, but as arrangements to gather a substantial amount of that data failed, it became less of a focus. The data gathered helped inform context, but did not merit a larger part of the study's narrative.

I interviewed and observed four of the participants at home. Nine were interviewed at school and via e-mail. Also, interviews with Angela, Julia, and family members of four of the participants provided opportunities to check interpretations and gain fuller understandings of the participants. With the home visits, I wanted to gain a sense of the participants' literate environments and to talk with them about specific literacies they pursued at home.

REFERENCES

Addison, Joanne, and Sharon James McGee. 2010. "Writing in High School / Writing in College: Research Trends and Future Directions." *College Composition and Communication* 62 (1): 147–79.

Adler-Kassner, Linda, and Heidi Estrem. 2007. "Reading Practices in the Writing Classroom." *WPA: Writing Program Administration* 31 (1–2): 35–47.

Adler-Kassner, Linda, and Susanmarie Harrington. 2002. *Basic Writing as a Political Act: Public Conversations about Writing and Literacies.* Cresskill, NJ: Hampton Press.

Agger, Ben. 2004. *Speeding Up Fast Capitalism: Cultures, Jobs, Families, Schools, Bodies.* Boulder, CO: Paradigm.

Anderson, Virginia. 2010. "Supply-Side Dreams: Composition, Technology, and the Circular Logic of Class." *Computers and Composition* 27 (2): 124–37. http://dx.doi.org/10.1016/j.compcom.2010.03.002.

Anson, Chris M., and Robert A. Schwegler. 2012. "Tracking the Mind's Eye: A New Technology for Researching Twenty-First-Century Writing and Reading Processes." *College Composition and Communication* 64 (1): 151–71.

Arola, Kristin. 2010. "The Design of Web 2.0: The Rise of the Template, The Fall of Design." *Computers and Composition* 27 (1): 4–14. http://dx.doi.org /10.1016/j.compcom.2009.11.004.

Bakhtin, M. M. 1981. *The Dialogic Imagination: Four Essays.* Trans. Caryl Emerson and Michael Holquist. Austin: University of Texas Press.

Banks, Adam J. 2006. *Race, Rhetoric, and Technology: Searching for Higher Ground.* Mahwah, NJ: Lawrence Erlbaum.

Bartholomae, David. 1985. "Inventing the University." In *When a Writer Can't Write: Studies in Writer's Block and Other Composing-Process Problems*, ed. Mike Rose, 134–65. New York: Guilford Press.

Bartholomae, David, and Anthony Petrosky, eds. 1986. *Facts, Artifacts, and Counterfacts: Theory and Method for a Reading and Writing Course.* Upper Montclair, NJ: Boynton/Cook.

Barton, David, and Mary Hamilton. 1998. *Local Literacies: Reading and Writing in One Community.* London: Routledge. http://dx.doi.org/10.4324/978020 3448885.

Bauerlein, Mark. 2008. *The Dumbest Generation: How the Digital Age Stupefies Young Americans and Jeopardizes Our Future (or, Don't Trust Anyone under 30).* New York, NY: Penguin.

Berthoff, Ann. 1981. *The Making of Meaning: Metaphors, Models, and Maxims for Writing Teachers.* Upper Montclair, N.J.: Boynton/Cook.

DOI: 10.7330/9780874219333.c008

Birkerts, Sven. 1994. *The Gutenberg Elegies: The Fate of Reading in an Electronic Age.* Boston: Faber and Faber.

Blair, Ann. Jan 2003. "Reading Strategies for Coping with Information Overload ca. 1550–1700." *Journal of the History of Ideas* 64 (1): 11–28. Medline:12841169

Bolter, Jay David, and Richard Grusin. 2000. *Remediation: Understanding New Media.* Cambridge, MA: MIT Press.

Bosley, Lisa. 2008. "'I Don't Teach Reading': Critical Reading Instruction in Composition Courses." *Literacy Research and Instruction* 47 (4): 285–308. http://dx.doi.org/10.1080/19388070802332861.

boyd, danah. 2008. "Why Youth (Heart) Social Network Sites: The Role of Networked Publics in Teenage Social Life." In *Youth, Identity, and Digital Media,* ed. David Buckingham, 119–42. Cambridge, MA: MIT Press.

Brandt, Deborah. 1995. "Accumulating Literacy: Writing and Learning to Write in the Twentieth Century." *College English* 57 (6): 649–68. http://dx.doi.org/10.2307/378570.

Brandt, Deborah. 2004. "Drafting U.S. Literacy." *College English* 66 (5): 485–502. http://dx.doi.org/10.2307/4140731.

Brandt, Deborah. 2009. *Literacy and Learning: Reflections on Writing, Reading, and Society.* San Francisco, CA: Jossey-Bass.

Brandt, Deborah, and Katie Clinton. 2002. "Limits of the Local: Expanding Perspectives on Literacy as a Social Practice." *Journal of Literacy Research* 34 (3): 337–56. http://dx.doi.org/10.1207/s15548430jlr3403_4.

Brent, Doug. 1992. *Reading as Rhetorical Invention: Knowledge, Persuasion, and the Teaching of Research-Based Writing.* Urbana, IL: NCTE Press.

Brodkey, Linda. 1986. "Tropics of Literacy." *Journal of Education* 168 (2): 47–54.

Brooke, Robert. 1988. "Modeling a Writer's Identity: Reading and Imitation in the Writing Classroom." *College Composition and Communication* 39 (1): 23–41. http://dx.doi.org/10.2307/357814.

Buckingham, David, and Julian Sefton-Green. 1994. *Cultural Studies Goes to School: Reading and Teaching Popular Media.* London: Taylor & Francis.

Butler, Paul. 2008. *Out of Style: Reanimating Stylistic Study in Composition and Rhetoric.* Logan, UT: Utah State University Press.

Carr, Nicholas. 2010. *The Shallows: What the Internet Is Doing to Our Brains.* New York: W.W. Norton.

Carroll, Lee Ann. 2002. *Rehearsing New Roles: How College Students Develop as Writers.* Carbondale: Southern Illinois University Press.

Castells, Manuel. 2010. *The Rise of the Network Society.* 2nd ed. Vol. 1. Chichester, West Sussex: Wiley-Blackwell.

Charney, Davida. 1993. "A Study in Rhetorical Reading: How Evolutionists Read 'The Spandrels of San Marco." In *Understanding Scientific Prose,* ed. Jack Selzer, 203–31. Madison: University of Wisconsin Press.

Coiro, Julie, and Elizabeth Dobler. 2007. "Exploring the Online Reading Comprehension Strategies Used by Sixth-Grade Skilled Readers to Search for and Locate Information on the Internet." *Reading Research Quarterly* 42 (2): 214–57. http://dx.doi.org/10.1598/RRQ.42.2.2.

Collins, James, and Richard K. Blot. 2003. *Literacy and Literacies: Texts, Power, and Identity.* New York: Cambridge University Press. http://dx.doi.org/10.1017/CBO9780511486661.

Cope, Bill, and Mary Kalantzis, eds. 2000. *Multiliteracies: Literacy Learning and the Design of Social Futures.* London: Taylor and Francis.

Corbett, Edward P. J. 1971. "The Theory and Practice of Imitation in Classical Rhetoric." *College Composition and Communication* 22 (3): 243–50. http://dx.doi .org/10.2307/356450.

Cummings, Robert E. 2009. *Lazy Virtues: Teaching Writing in the Age of Wikipedia.* Nashville, TN: Vanderbilt University Press.

D'Angelo, Frank. 1973. "Imitation and Style." *College Composition and Communication* 24 (3): 283–90. http://dx.doi.org/10.2307/356855.

De Aenlle, Conrad. 2009. "Digital Archivists, Now in Demand." *New York Times,* February 7. http://www.nytimes.com/2009/02/08/jobs/08starts.html?_r=0

Delpit, Lisa. 1995. *Other People's Children: Cultural Conflict in the Classroom.* New York: New Press.

Denscombe, Martyn. 2007. *The Good Research Guide: For Small-scale Social Research Projects.* Maidenhead: Open UP.

Devitt, Amy J. 2004. *Writing Genres.* Carbondale: Southern Illinois University Press.

DeWitt, Scott Lloyd. 2001. *Writing Inventions: Identities, Technologies, Pedagogies.* Albany, NY: State University of New York Press.

Diogenes, Marvin, and Andrea Lunsford. 2006. "Toward Delivering New Definitions of Writing." In *Delivering College Composition: The Fifth Canon,* ed. Kathleen Blake Yancey, 141–54. Portsmouth, NH: Heinemann/Boynton Cook.

Donahue, Patricia, and Ellen Quandahl, eds. 1989. *Reclaiming Pedagogy: The Rhetoric of the Classroom.* Carbondale: Southern Illinois University Press.

Dubisar, Abby, and Jason Palmeri. 2010. "Palin / Pathos / Peter Griffin: Political Video Remix and Composition Pedagogy." *Computers and Composition* 27 (2): 77–93. http://dx.doi.org/10.1016/j.compcom.2010.03.004.

Dux, Paul E., Michael N. Tombu, Stephenie Harrison, Baxter P. Rogers, Frank Tong, and René Marois. 16 Jul, 2009. "Training Improves Multitasking Performance by Increasing the Speed of Information Processing in Human Prefrontal Cortex." *Neuron* 63 (1): 127–38. http://dx.doi.org/10.1016/j .neuron.2009.06.005. Medline:19607798

Dyson, Anne Haas, and Celia Genishi. 2005. *On the Case: Approaches to Language and Literacy Research.* New York: Teachers College/NCRLL.

Edmundson, Mark. 2004. *Why Read?* New York: Bloomsbury Publishing.

Eisenstein, Elizabeth L. 2011. *Divine Art, Infernal Machine: The Reception of Printing in the West from First Impressions to the Sense of an Ending.* Philadelphia: University of Pennsylvania Press.

Elbow, Peter. 1973. *Writing without Teachers.* New York: Oxford University Press.

Elbow, Peter. 1993. "The War Between Reading and Writing—and How to End It." *Rhetoric Review* 12 (1): 5–24. http://dx.doi.org/10.1080/07350199309389024.

Ellison, Katherine E. 2006. *Fatal News: Reading and Information Overload in Early Eighteenth-century Literature.* New York: Routledge.

Evans, Ellen, and Jeanne Po. 2007. "A Break in the Transaction: Examining Students' Responses to Digital Texts." *Computers and Composition* 24 (1): 56–73. http://dx.doi.org/10.1016/j.compcom.2006.12.003.

Faigley, Lester. 2006. "Rhetorics Fast and Slow." In *Rhetorical Agendas: Political, Ethical, Spiritual,* ed. Patricia Bizzell, 3–9. Mahwah, NJ: Erlbaum.

Farmer, Frank M., and Phillip K. Arrington. 1993. "Apologies and Accommodations: Imitation and the Writing Process." *Rhetoric Society Quarterly* 23 (1): 12–34. http://dx.doi.org/10.1080/02773949309390976.

Flower, Linda. 1988. "The Construction of Purpose in Writing and Reading." *College English* 50 (5): 528–50. http://dx.doi.org/10.2307/377490.

Flower, Linda, and John R. Hayes. 1981. "A Cognitive Process Theory of Writing." *College Composition and Communication* 32 (4): 365–87. http://dx.doi.org/10.2307/356600.

Foertsch, Julie. 1995. "Where Cognitive Psychology Applies: How Theories About Memory and Transfer Can Influence Composition Pedagogy." *Written Communication* 12 (3): 360–83. http://dx.doi.org/10.1177/0741088395012003006.

Gallagher, Kelly. 2009. *Readicide: How Schools Are Killing Reading and What You Can Do about It.* Portland, ME: Stenhouse.

Garrett, R. Kelly, and James N. Danziger. 2007. "IM = Interruption Management? Instant Messaging and Disruption in the Workplace." *Journal of Computer-Mediated Communication* 13 (1): 23–42. http://dx.doi.org/10.1111/j.1083-6101.2007.00384.x.

Gee, James. 2004. *Situated Language and Learning: A Critique of Traditional Schooling.* New York: Routledge.

George, Diana. 2002. "From Analysis to Design: Visual Communication in the Teaching of Writing." *College Composition and Communication* 54 (1): 11–39. http://dx.doi.org/10.2307/1512100.

Gleick, James. 1999. *Faster: The Acceleration of Just about Everything.* New York: Pantheon.

Goggin, Peter. 2008. *Professing Literacy in Composition Studies.* Cresskill, NJ: Hampton Press.

Graff, Gerald, and Cathy Birkenstein. 2006. *They Say / I Say: The Moves That Matter in Academic Writing.* New York: W. W. Norton & Company.

Graff, Harvey J. 1987. *The Legacies of Literacy: Continuities and Contradictions in Western Culture and Society.* Bloomington, IN: Indiana University Press.

Green, Angela. 2009. "The Politics of Literacy: Countering the Rhetoric of Accountability in the Spellings Report and Beyond." *College Composition and Communication* 61 (1): W367–84.

Guillory, John. 2010. "Close Reading: Prologue and Epilogue." *ADE Bulletin* 149: 8–14. http://dx.doi.org/10.1632/ade.149.8.

Hansen, Kristine, and Christine Farris. 2010. "Introduction: The 'Taking Care of' Business." In *College Credit for Writing in High School: The "taking-care-of" Business,* ed. Kristine Hansen and Christine Farris, xvii–xxxiii. Urbana, IL: NCTE Press.

Harkin, Patricia. 2005. "The Reception of Reader-Response Theory." *College Composition and Communication* 56 (3): 410–25.

Harklau, Linda. 2001. "From High School to College: Student Perspectives on Literacy Practices." *Journal of Literacy Research* 33 (1): 33–70. http://dx.doi.org/10.1080/10862960109548102.

Hassan, Robert. 2009. *Empires of Speed: Time and the Acceleration of Politics and Society.* Leiden: Brill. http://dx.doi.org/10.1163/ej.9789004175907.i-254.

Hayes, John R. 2001. "A New Framework for Understanding Cognition and Affect in Writing." In *Literacy: A Critical Sourcebook,* ed. Ellen Cushman,

Eugene R. Kintgen, Barry Kroll, and Mike Rose, 172–98. Boston: Bedford/ St. Martin's.

Hayles, Katherine. 2007. "Hyper and Deep Attention: The Generational Divide in Cognitive Modes." *Profession* 13 (1): 187–99. http://dx.doi.org/10.1632/prof .2007.2007.1.187.

Heath, Joseph, and Andrew Potter. 2004. *Nation of Rebels: Why Counterculture Became Consumer Culture.* New York: HarperBusiness.

Heath, Shirley Brice. 1983. *Ways with Words: Language, Life, and Work in Communities and Classrooms.* New York, Cambridge: Cambridge University Press.

Helmers, Marguerite. 2003. "Introduction: Representing Reading." In *Intertexts: Reading Pedagogy in College Writing Classrooms,* ed. Marguerite Helmers, 3–26. Mahwah, NJ: Lawrence Erlbaum.

Henry, Jeanne. 2009. "Cultivating Reading Workshop: New Theory into New Practice." *Open Words: Access and English Studies* 3 (1): 62–74.

Hesse, Doug. 2010. "Interchanges: Response to Cynthia L. Selfe's 'The Movement of Air, the Breath of Meaning: Aurality and Multimodal Composing.'" *College Composition and Communication* 61 (3): 602–5.

Howard, Rebecca Moore. 1999. *Standing in the Shadow of Giants: Plagiarists, Authors, Collaborators.* Stamford, CT: Ablex Publishing Corporation.

Howard, Rebecca Moore, Tricia Serviss, and Tanya K. Rodrigue. 2010. "Writing from Sources, Writing from Sentences." *Writing & Pedagogy* 2 (2): 177–92.

Hoy, Pat, II. 2009. "Healing Conceptual Blindness." *Rhetoric Review* 28 (3): 304–24. http://dx.doi.org/10.1080/07350190902958933.

Hruby, George, and Usha Goswami. 2011. "Neuroscience and Reading: A Review for Reading Education Researchers." *Reading Research Quarterly* 46 (2): 156–72. http://dx.doi.org/10.1598/RRQ.46.2.4.

Hull, Glynda, and Mike Rose. 1990. "'This Wooden Shack Place': The Logic of an Unconventional Reading." *College Composition and Communication* 41 (3): 287–98. http://dx.doi.org/10.2307/357656.

Jack, Jordynn, and L. Gregory Appelbaum. 2010. "'This is Your Brain on Rhetoric': Research Directions for Neurorhetorics." *Rhetoric Society Quarterly* 40 (5): 411–37. http://dx.doi.org/10.1080/02773945.2010.516303.

Jenkins, Henry. 1992. *Textual Poachers: Television Fans & Participatory Culture.* New York: Routledge.

Jenkins, Henry. 2008. *Convergence Culture: Where Old and New Media Collide.* New York: New York University Press.

Jenkins, Henry, Katie Clinton, Ravi Purushotma, Alice J. Robison, and Margaret Weigel. 2006. "Confronting the Challenges of Participatory Culture: Media Education for the 21st Century." Chicago, IL: The MacArthur Foundation. http://www.macfound.org/programs/learning/

Johnson, Steven. 2010. *Where Good Ideas Come From: The Natural History of Innovation.* New York: Riverhead.

Johnson, T. R. 2003. *A Rhetoric of Pleasure: Prose Style and Today's Composition Classroom.* Portsmouth, NH: Boynton/Cook.

Jolliffe, David A. 2003. "Who is Teaching Composition Students to Read and How Are They Doing It?" *Composition Studies* 31 (1): 127–42.

Jolliffe, David A, and Allison Harl. 2008. "Studying the 'Reading Transition' from High School to College." *College English* 70 (6): 599–617.

Kraemer, Don. 2007. "The Economy of Explicit Instruction." *Journal of Basic Writing* 26 (2): 95–116.

Kress, Gunther. 2003. *Literacy in the New Media Age.* London: Routledge. http://dx.doi.org/10.4324/9780203164754.

Langer, Judith, and Sheila Flihan. 2000. "Writing and Reading Relationships: Constructive Tasks." In *Perspectives on Writing,* ed. Roselmina Indrisano and James R. Squire, 112–39. Newark, DE: International Reading Association.

Lanham, Richard A. 2006. *The Economics of Attention: Style and Substance in the Age of Information.* Chicago: University of Chicago Press.

Lankshear, Colin, and Michele Knobel. 2003. *New Literacies: Changing Knowledge and Classroom Learning.* Buckingham: Open University Press.

Lenhart, Amanda, Sousan Arafeh, Aaron Smith, and Alexandra Macgill. 2008. *Writing, Technology and Teens.* Pew Internet and American Life Project and National Commission on Writing, April 24. http://pewinternet.org/Reports/2008/Writing-Technology-and-Teens.aspx.

Lenhart, Amanda, Kristen Purcell, Aaron Smith, and Kathryn Zickuhr. 2010. *Social Media and Young Adults.* Pew Internet and American Life Project, February 3. http://www.pewinternet.org/Reports/2010/Social-Media-and-Young-Adults.aspx.

Lessig, Lawrence. 2008. *Remix: Making Art and Commerce Thrive in the Hybrid Economy.* New York: Penguin. http://dx.doi.org/10.5040/9781849662505.

Lewin, Elisabeth. 2008. "Scott Sigler Talks about Social Media, Podcast Books and the Future of Publishing." Podcasting News, August 22. http://www.podcastingnews.com/content/2008/08/scott-sigler-talks-about-social-media-podcast-books-and-the-future-of-publishing/ (site discontinued).

Lin, Lin, Tip Robertson, and Jennifer Lee. 2009. "Reading Performances Between Novices and Experts in Different Media Multitasking Environments." *Computers in the Schools* 26 (3): 169–86. http://dx.doi.org/10.1080/07380560903095162.

Lindemann, Erika. 1993. "Freshman Composition: No Place for Literature." *College English* 55 (3): 311–6. http://dx.doi.org/10.2307/378743.

Littau, Karin. 2006. *Theories of Reading: Books, Bodies, and Bibliomania.* Cambridge and Malden, MA: Polity Press.

Lohr, Steve. 2011. "When There's No Such Thing as Too Much Information." *New York Times,* April 23. http://www.nytimes.com/2011/04/24/business/24unboxed.html.

Macrorie, Ken. 1970. *Telling Writing.* Rochelle Park, N.J.: Hayden.

McCabe, David P., and Alan D. Castel. Apr 2008. "Seeing is Believing: The Effect of Brain Images on Judgments of Scientific Reasoning." *Cognition* 107 (1): 343–52. http://dx.doi.org/10.1016/j.cognition.2007.07.017. Medline:17803985

McCormick, Kathleen. 1994. *The Culture of Reading and the Teaching of English.* Manchester: Manchester University Press.

Micciche, Laura R. 2007. *Doing Emotion: Rhetoric, Writing, Teaching.* Portsmouth, NH: Boynton/Cook.

Miller, Richard. 2010. "Distraction versus Wandering." *text2cloud,* November 17. http://text2cloud.com/2010/11/distraction-versus-wandering/

National Endowment for the Arts (NEA). 2009. *Reading on the Rise: A New Chapter in American Literacy.* http://www.nea.gov.

Newkirk, Thomas. 2009. *Holding on to Good Ideas in a Time of Bad Ones: Six Literacy Principles worth Fighting for.* Portsmouth, NH: Heinemann.

Newkirk, Thomas. 2012. *The Art of Slow Reading: Six Time-honored Practices for Engagement.* Portsmouth, NH: Heinemann.

Nunberg, Geoffrey. 1996. "Farewell to the Information Age." In *The Future of the Book,* ed. Geoffrey Nunberg, 103–38. Berkeley: University of California Press.

Nyhan, Brendan. 2010. "Why the 'Death Panel' Myth Wouldn't Die: Misinformation in the Health Care Reform Debate." *Forum* 8 (1): 1–24.

Ong, Walter J. 1972. "Media Transformation: The Talked Book." *College English* 34 (3): 405–10. http://dx.doi.org/10.2307/375143.

Ophir, Eyal, Clifford Nass, and Anthony D. Wagner. 15 Sep, 2009. "Cognitive Control in Media Multitaskers." *Proceedings of the National Academy of Sciences of the United States of America* 106 (37): 15583–7. http://dx.doi.org/10.1073/pnas.0903620106. Medline:19706386

Pajares, Frank. 2003. "Self-efficacy Beliefs, Motivation, and Achievement in Writing: A Review of The Literature." *Reading & Writing Quarterly* 19 (2): 139–58. http://dx.doi.org/10.1080/10573560308222.

Petersen, Bruce T. 1982. "Writing about Responses: A Unified Model of Reading, Interpretation, and Composition." *College English* 44 (5): 459–68. http://dx.doi.org/10.2307/376649.

Petrosky, Anthony J. 1982. "From Story to Essay: Reading and Writing." *College Composition and Communication* 33 (1): 19–36. http://dx.doi.org/10.2307/357842.

Porter, James E. 1986. "Intertextuality and the Discourse Community." *Rhetoric Review* 5 (1): 34–47. http://dx.doi.org/10.1080/07350198609359131.

Porter, James E. 2009. "Recovering Delivery for Digital Rhetoric." *Computers and Composition* 26 (4): 207–24. http://dx.doi.org/10.1016/j.compcom.2009.09.004.

Porter, James E. 2010. "Rhetoric in (as) a Digital Economy." In *Rhetorics and Technologies: New Directions in Writing and Communication,* ed. Stuart A. Selber, 173–97. Columbia, SC: University of South Carolina Press.

Postman, Neil. 1986. *Amusing Ourselves to Death: Public Discourse in the Age of Show Business.* New York: Penguin.

Powell, Annette Harris. 2007. "Access(ing), Habits, Attitudes, and Engagements: Re-Thinking Access as Practice." *Computers and Composition* 24 (1): 16–35. http://dx.doi.org/10.1016/j.compcom.2006.12.006.

Pressley, Michael. 2002. *Reading Instruction That Works: The Case for Balanced Teaching.* New York: Guilford Press.

Purcell-Gates, Victoria. 2012. "Epistemological Tensions in Reading Research and a Vision for the Future." *Reading Research Quarterly* 47 (4): 465–71.

Qualley, Donna. 1993. "Using Reading in the Writing Classroom." In *Nuts and Bolts: A Practical Guide to Teaching College Composition,* ed. Thomas Newkirk, 101–27. Portsmouth: Boynton/Cook.

Reder, Stephen, and Erica Davila. 2005. "Context and Literacy Practices." *Annual Review of Applied Linguistics* 25:170–87. http://dx.doi.org/10.1017/S0267190505000097.

Reiff, Mary Jo, and Anis Bawarshi. 2011. "Tracing Discursive Resources: How Students Use Prior Genre Knowledge to Negotiate New Writing Contexts in First-Year Composition." *Written Communication* 28 (3): 312–37. http://dx.doi.org/10.1177/0741088311410183.

Richtel, Matt. 2010. "Growing Up Digital, Wired for Distraction." *New York Times*, November 21. http://www.nytimes.com/2010/11/21/technology/21brain.html.

Rideout, Victoria, Ulla Foehr, and Donald Roberts. 2010. "Generation M2: Media in the Lives of 8- to 18-Year-Olds." *The Henry J. Kaiser Family Foundation*, January 20. http://kff.org/other/event/generation-m2-media-in-the-lives-of/

Ridolfo, Jim, and Dànielle Nicole DeVoss. 2009. "Composing for Recomposition: Rhetorical Velocity and Delivery." *Kairos* 13.2 http://www.technorhetoric.net/13.2/topoi/ridolfo_devoss/

Rogers, Rebecca. 2003. *A Critical Discourse Analysis of Family Literacy Practices: Power in and out of Print*. Mahwah, NJ: L. Erlbaum.

Rosen, Christine. 2008. "The Myth of Multitasking." *The New Atlantis - A Journal of Technology & Society*. http://www.thenewatlantis.com/publications/the-myth-of-multitasking.

Rosenberg, Daniel. 2003. "Early Modern Information Overload." *Journal of the History of Ideas* 64 (1): 1–9. http://dx.doi.org/10.1353/jhi.2003.0017.

Salmeron, Ladislao, Jose Canas, Walter Kintsch, and Inmaculada Fajardo. 2005. "Reading Strategies and Hypertext Comprehension." *Discourse Processes* 40 (3): 171–91. http://dx.doi.org/10.1207/s15326950dp4003_1.

Salvatori, Mariolina. 1983. "Reading and Writing a Text: Correlations between Reading and Writing Patterns." *College English* 45 (7): 657–66. http://dx.doi.org/10.2307/377175.

Salvatori, Mariolina. 1996. "Conversations with Texts: Reading in the Teaching of Composition." *College English* 58 (4): 440–54. http://dx.doi.org/10.2307/378854.

Salvatori, Mariolina, and Patricia Donahue. 2012. "Stories about Reading: Appearance, Disappearance, Morphing, and Revival." *College English* 75 (2): 199–217.

Salvucci, Dario D., and Niels A. Taatgen. Jan 2008. "Threaded Cognition: An Integrated Theory of Concurrent Multitasking." *Psychological Review* 115 (1): 101–30. http://dx.doi.org/10.1037/0033-295X.115.1.101. Medline:18211187

Selber, Stuart. 2004. *Multiliteracies for a Digital Age*. Carbondale: Southern Illinois UP.

Selfe, Cynthia L, ed. 2007. *Multimodal Composition: Resources for Teachers*. Cresskill, NJ: Hampton Press.

Selfe, Cynthia L. 2009. "The Movement of Air, the Breath of Meaning: Aurality and Multimodal Composing." *College Composition and Communication* 60 (4): 616–63.

Selfe, Cynthia L. 2010. "Response to Doug Hesse." *College Composition and Communication* 61 (3): 606–10.

Sendlor, Charles. 2011. "FanFiction.Net Fandoms: Story and Traffic Statistics." *Fan Fiction Statistics*, January 11. http://ffnresearch.blogspot.com/2011/01/fanfictionnet-fandoms-story-and-traffic.html.

Shannon, Patrick, and Kenneth Goodman. 2011. "Reading Around Reading Education: Trying to Understand Federal Policy Change." *Journal of Reading Education* 36 (2): 5–10.

Simon, Herbert. 1971. "Designing Organizations for an Information-rich World." In *Computers, Communications and the Public Interest*, ed. Martin Greenberger, 37–72. Baltimore, MD: Johns Hopkins University Press.

Sosnoski, James. 1999. "Hyper-readers and Their Reading Engines." In *Passions, Pedagogies, and 21st Century Technologies*, ed. Gail E. Hawisher and Cynthia L. Selfe, 161–77. Logan: Utah State University Press.

Sternglass, Marilyn S. 1997. *Time to Know Them: a Longitudinal Study of Writing and Learning at the College Level.* Mahwah, NJ: Lawrence Erlbaum Associates.

Strasma, Kip. 2001. "Emerging Pedagogy: Teaching Digital Hypertexts in Social Contexts." *Computers and Composition* 18 (3): 257–74. http://dx.doi .org/10.1016/S8755-4615(01)00055-X.

Strasma, Kip. 2010. "Reading Hypertext New Media." In *RAW (Reading and Writing) New Media*, ed. Cheryl E. Ball and James Kalmbach, 183–96. Cresskill, NJ: Hampton Press.

Street, Brian V. 1995. *Social Literacies: Critical Approaches to Literacy in Development, Ethnography and Education.* London: Longman.

Street, Brian V. 2003. "What's 'new' in New Literacy Studies? Critical Approaches to Literacy in Theory and Practice." *Current Issues in Comparative Education* 5 (2): 77–91.

Street, Brian V., and Joanna Street. 1995. "The Schooling of Literacy." In Street, Brian V., *Social Literacies: Critical Approaches to Literacy in Development, Ethnography and Education*, 106–131. London: Longman.

Stuckey, J. Elspeth. 1991. *The Violence of Literacy.* Portsmouth, NH: Boynton/ Cook.

Supovitz, Jonathan. 2009. "Can High Stakes Testing Leverage Educational Improvement? Prospects From the Last Decade of Testing and Accountability Reform." *Journal of Educational Change* 10 (2–3): 211–27. http://dx.doi.org /10.1007/s10833-009-9105-2.

Tate, Gary. 1993. "A Place for Literature in Freshman Composition." *College English* 55 (3): 317–21. http://dx.doi.org/10.2307/378744.

Thill, Scott. 2009. "Kutiman's *ThruYou* Mashup Turns YouTube Into Funk Machine." *Wired*, March 25. http://www.wired.com/underwire/2009/03 /kutimans-pionee/

Tyack, David B., and Larry Cuban. 1995. *Tinkering toward Utopia: A Century of Public School Reform.* Cambridge, MA: Harvard University Press.

University College London. 2007. "Work Package IV: Student Information-Seeking Behaviour in Context." British Library and JISC, June 22. http:// www.ucl.ac.uk/infostudies/research/ciber/downloads/

Wardle, Elizabeth. 2007. "Understanding 'Transfer' from FYC: Preliminary Results of a Longitudinal Study." *WPA: Writing Program Administration* 31 (1–2): 65–85.

Weisberg, Deena Skolnick, Frank C. Keil, Joshua Goodstein, Elizabeth Rawson, and Jeremy R. Gray. Mar 2008. "The Seductive Allure of Neuroscience Expla-nations." *Journal of Cognitive Neuroscience* 20 (3): 470–7. http://dx.doi.org /10.1162/jocn.2008.20040. Medline:18004955

Welch, Kathleen E. 1999. *Electric Rhetoric: Classical Rhetoric, Oralism, and a New Literacy.* Cambridge, MA: MIT Press.

Welch, Nancy. 2011. "'We're Here, and We're Not Going Anywhere': Why Working-Class Rhetorical Traditions Still Matter." *College English* 73 (3): 221–42.

Westbrook, Steve. 2006. "Visual Rhetoric in a Culture of Fear: Impediments to Multimedia Production." *College English* 68 (5): 457–80. http://dx.doi.org /10.2307/25472166.

Williams, Bronwyn T. 2009. *Shimmering Literacies: Popular Culture & Reading & Writing Online.* New York: Peter Lang.

Yagelski, Robert. 2000. *Literacy Matters: Writing and Reading the Social Self.* New York: Teachers College.

Yancey, Kathleen Blake. 2004. "Made Not Only in Words: Composition in a New Key." *College Composition and Communication* 56 (2): 297–328. http://dx.doi .org/10.2307/4140651.

Zhang, Shenglan, and Nell Duke. 2008. "Strategies for Internet Reading with Different Reading Purposes: A Descriptive Study of Twelve Good Internet Readers." *Journal of Literacy Research* 40 (1): 128–62. http://dx.doi.org/10 .1080/10862960802070491.

ABOUT THE AUTHOR

DANIEL KELLER is an assistant professor of English at The Ohio State University at Newark, where he teaches composition, digital media, and literacy studies. His work has been published in *The Writing Center Journal* and edited collections on digital literacy. He earned his PhD in rhetoric and composition at the University of Louisville.

INDEX